Seven Stages

OTHER BOOKS BY

GEOFFREY TREASE

The Seven Queens of England
Seven Kings of England
Sir Walter Raleigh
Cue for Treason
Message to Hadrian
Web of Traitors
The Silken Secret
Victory at Valmy
Follow My Black Plume
Escape to King Alfred

GEOFFREY TREASE

Seven Stages

Illustrated with Photographs

NEW YORK

THE VANGUARD PRESS, INC.

Author's Foreword

Why seven 'stages'? Because there is no one convenient word for everybody who works in the theatre, whether as playwright or composer, producer or manager, actor, singer or dancer.

Why the particular seven great figures of the theatre whose lives are chronicled in these pages? First, because they represent between them all the various functions listed above. Secondly, because these three women and four men, English and French, Italian and Russian and Swedish, remind us that the stage-door stands open to both sexes and all nationalities. Thirdly, these seven life stories link up to give us an outline of theatrical history at all its greatest and most colourful periods: our famous characters are seen against famous settings – the Elizabethan playhouse, the Paris and Versailles of Louis the Fourteenth, Drury Lane in the eighteenth century, Covent Garden and the Lyceum in the nineteenth, La Scala during the heroic age of the Italian struggle for freedom, and the Imperial Ballet at St Petersburg under the last Tsar. But perhaps the best reason of all for selecting these seven great men and women is that they were interesting human beings and that things happened to them outside the theatre as well as inside.

Contents

Illustrations

1. The Mystery of Marlowe

What sort of man was this Christopher Marlowe? What do we know about him?

Those were the questions in the coroner's mind one summer's day in 1593 – and in the minds of the jurymen as they shuffled back into their places, grim-faced after viewing the body.

There were so many strange tales going about. The dead man had been in trouble before. He held dangerous, shocking views. It was said that he had done secret service for the Queen in foreign parts. He had friends in high places – people like Ralegh and the Walsinghams – yet there were ugly whispers of treason. A warrant for his arrest had been issued by the Privy Council only two weeks ago, yet at the time of his death he was going about openly, a free man.

Witnesses spoke of a tavern brawl, a little argument over the bill, daggers drawn suddenly in anger. . . . A common enough incident in Tudor London – but was there more in it than met the eye?

True, the man had neither wife nor child and nobody seemed particularly affected by his death. True, the plague was raging in the city, and with scores of respectable folk dying every week, the passing of one disreputable young stranger, probably through his own fault, was of no great concern. But the law was the law, the Queen's peace must be kept, and a man could not be killed like this without questions being asked.

Four centuries later, questions are still being asked.

Once the dead man was laid to rest in the churchyard of St Nicholas at Deptford, only the fading memories of his friends and enemies could recall his features. If anyone had ever thought it worth while to paint his portrait, it had been done in earlier days when he was at Cambridge. His old college has the portrait of a young man which was quite recently discovered and claimed by some people to be Marlowe's. There is no certainty. The most that can be said is that the age and the date fit. Cambridge was very small in those days, with only a few hundred scholars distributed among over a dozen colleges, so that Corpus Christi would have had a mere handful of members of exactly the same age and year as Marlowe.

He was born in the ancient city of Canterbury, probably on 6 February 1564 (his christening was recorded on the 26th) so that he was about two months older than Shakespeare. His father, John Marlowe, was a shoemaker. His mother, Catherine, was the daughter of a clergyman who had been turned out of his parish some years before, during the brief reign of Queen Mary, when the Roman Catholic faith was temporarily restored. Christopher had an elder sister, Mary. Later he had younger brothers and sisters, but the boys died, and he grew up as the only son among four girls.

Canterbury was a town of narrow streets and winding lanes. Half-timbered gables leant towards each other like overhanging cliffs. There were inns with galleried court-yards and stone churches with leering gargoyles. Curfew sounded every evening from the great Bell Harry Tower of the cathedral.

The pilgrims described in Chaucer's *Canterbury Tales* now came no more. All that had stopped with the Reformation. Middle-aged people still recalled with sorrow and anger (though they had to be careful what they said) how King Henry the Eighth's Commissioners had stripped the wonderful shrine of the martyred Arch-bishop Thomas à. Becket and made off with all its treasures. But, though the busy pilgrim traffic had gone for ever, Canterbury was a prosperous and lively place. Half-way between Dover and London, it was a natural halt for people travelling to and from the Continent. Foreign ambassadors and even visiting royalties stayed in Canterbury, filling the inns with splendid clothes and out-landish accents. Such travellers may have given the shoe-maker's small boy those first romantic glimpses of the outside world which were to feed his fancy and that love of pomp and pageantry which spills over in his plays. When he was nine he must certainly have witnessed some magnificent shows and parades, for in that year Queen Elizabeth paid a long visit to Canterbury and celebrated her birthday there.

Nobody knows how a poet is made. We can only guess

at the influences which helped to shape Christopher Marlowe into one of the immortals of English literature.

Where, for instance, did he collect that powerful, glittering vocabulary which was to pour out like molten metal in his verses – making them sometimes unforgettable poetry, sometimes turgid nonsense, but hardly ever flat or colourless? There were comparatively few books and none specially written for young readers. There was no dictionary, no encyclopaedia. Neither English literature nor English composition was taught in school. Latin, and above all Latin grammar, hammered in by the dullest methods, formed the main part of education.

Perhaps the luckiest thing for Christopher's poetic development was that he did not enter the grammar school until an unusually late age. No one knows where he got his earlier lessons, but he could scarcely have missed much of value by not starting sooner on the rigorous timetable of a Tudor grammar school.

The King's School at Canterbury claims to be the oldest in England. It had been reformed by Henry the Eighth and, though it had pupils from many well-to-do families, it was open to anyone of ability. Archbishop Cranmer had made that point clear. 'If the gentleman's son be apt to learning, let him be admitted,' he ruled. 'If not, let the poor man's apt child enter his room' (or, in modern language, take his place).

Boys were normally accepted between the ages of nine and fifteen. Christopher got in by the skin of his teeth – we do not know why. He did not win his scholarship until the end of 1578 and when he first put on his black scholar's gown and presented himself at the school it was 14 January, with the dead-line of his fifteenth birthday only three weeks away.

Life for the next two years was largely Latin, but there was some relief from the grind. Out of class, boys could work off their energy by racing and wrestling, dancing and swimming, archery and (to quote one disapproving educationist of the time) the 'beastly fury and extreme violence' of football. And they could act in school plays.

It was a great age for play-acting, though as yet England had no great playwrights and the schoolmasters tended to look back down the ages for their material to ancient Roman authors like Terence and Seneca.

Plays were acted in the schools, at Oxford and Cambridge, and at the Inns of Court in London, where the law students formed something like a third university.

In the main towns, like Canterbury, the trade guilds still acted another type of play, just as they had done in the Middle Ages. They went round the streets with a procession of decorated carts which they called 'pageants' and used as open-air stages. Their scenes were based on Bible stories and each trade made itself responsible for an episode. In a city with enough different trades it was possible to act the whole story of mankind from Creation to Judgement Day.

Christopher had the chance to see yet a third kind of drama when the professional touring companies visited Canterbury and used one of the inn yards as a temporary theatre. They brought farcical comedy like *Gammer Gurton's Needle* and *Ralph Roister Doister*, old-fashioned moralities like *Hit Nail o' th' Head*, romances and melo-dramas like *The Solitary Knight* and *Murderous Michael*. England had a number of these troupes of strolling players, and the members must have been hard-working and versatile. One of their plays, Thomas Preston's *Lamentable Tragedy*, had thirty-eight speaking charac-ters, so arranged that they could be played by half a dozen men with a pair of boys to take care of all the feminine roles.

The literary standard of these plays was low. Some years later Shakespeare made fun of them in the play-scenes in *Hamlet* and *A Midsummer Night's Dream*. But the people, from the Queen downwards, enjoyed them thoroughly until something better was offered.

Just about the time Christopher Marlowe entered the King's School, a leading actor-manager named James Burbage decided that inn yards and makeshift stages were not good enough when he played in London. He put up a special building outside Bishopsgate and called it simply the Theatre. By the end of 1580, when Christopher left school, London had acquired two more such theatres. There was a boom in drama. The situation was ripe for the real dramatists.

For the present, though, the development of the London theatre was of no concern to young Marlowe. He was bound for Cambridge, where the King's School had a link with Corpus Christi, one of the oldest colleges, standing near the market place in the middle of the town.

Neither Oxford nor Cambridge was a very lively

intellectual centre at this date, but (as in most ages) they were lively enough in other ways. Robert Greene, another future playwright, who went up to Cambridge five years earlier, confessed afterwards that he had fallen into the bad company of 'wags as lewd as myself, with whom I consumed the flower of my youth'. John Lyly, also destined to write plays and fiction, warned parents against the perils awaiting their sons at Oxford: 'such playing at dice, such quaffing of drink, such dalliance with women, such dancing'. It is interesting to note that, in spite of all this, Lyly went on to Cambridge himself – and Greene moved over for a spell at Oxford. Marlowe was satisfied with only one university, but he spent six and a half years there, off and on, and probably acquired a taste for the sort of life he continued in London.

There are few records of his college life. He took his degree as Bachelor of Arts in 1584. He stayed on to take his further degree as Master – and this suggests that he was considered as a possible candidate for Holy Orders. It was soon clear, at least to himself, that he would never be happy as a clergyman in the Church of England. His mind was too independent, his utterances too shocking and irreverent, his habits too unconventional. At that particular moment in history all Europe was divided by an ideological barrier. 'Protestant' and 'Catholic' were not just religious labels but political ones. In Elizabeth's England, as in the countries beyond the Channel, the man who questioned the views of authority could lose his livelihood and even his life.

Something strange happened during Marlowe's closing

years at Cambridge. He was absent from the University a good deal. It was rumoured that he had been converted to the 'old religion' and that he had been abroad to Rheims, where there was a seminary for the training of English Catholics, who slipped back into England illegally and went about their work underground. It was 1587, the year which saw the execution of Mary, Queen of Scots, and the year before the Spanish Armada.

Marlowe was about to take his M.A. At the very last moment the University withheld the degree. And then occurred the remarkable thing. No less a body than the Queen's Privy Council stepped in. It passed the following resolution – the spelling of Marlowe's name is not important, for spelling in those days was not fixed and it was common for a name to appear in a variety of forms:

Whereas it was reported that Christopher Morley was determined to have gone beyond the seas to Reames and there to remain, Their Lordships thought good to certify that he had no such intent, but that in all his actions he had behaved himself orderly and discreetly, whereby he had done Her Majesty good service and deserved to be rewarded for his faithful dealing. Their Lordships' request was that the rumour thereof be allayed by all possible means, and that he should be furthered in the degree he was to take this next commencement: because it was not Her Majesty's pleasure that any one employed as he had been in matters touching the benefit of his country should be defamed by those that are ignorant in the affairs he went about.

What were those affairs? What had Marlowe been doing in Her Majesty's service? Shall we ever know?

The University bowed to the Privy Council's wishes. The degree was conferred. Christopher Marlowe, M.A., departed for London.

He was no stranger to the city. He must often have passed through it, travelling between Canterbury and Cambridge and on his mysterious missions for the Government. But now it was to be his home for the rest of his life.

London in 1587 was a sprawling, noisy, colourful, smelly place, spread along the muddy north bank of the Thames. The ancient walled city ran west from the grey-white fortress of the Tower, past St Paul's on its low hill, over the Fleet Ditch, to the rabbit-warren of lawyers called the Temple. Beyond this limit (Temple Bar) the road ran on along the 'Strand', lined with noblemen's mansions backing on to the river, until it reached the twin city of Westminster, with its abbey, its royal palace of Whitehall, and the remnant of an earlier palace used for meetings of Parliament. The population was already spreading far beyond even these areas. Men like Sir Thomas More had lived out at Chelsea. The first theatres were built outside the eastward boundaries. And on the other side of the river, reached by London Bridge or by one of the innumerable boats plying for hire, the old borough of Southwark was developing fast.

Marlowe was drawn at once into the world of the theatre.

Unlike Shakespeare, who arrived in London about the same time, he himself seems to have had no desire to act. It was the writing which appealed to him. At Cambridge he had written a not-very-good verse translation of the Roman poet Ovid, but, if nothing more, it had been a useful exercise in metre and vocabulary, and he must long have felt, listening to the crude plays of that period, that he could do better himself if he tried.

For another thing, the theatre represented everything that was new and daring and opposed to the stuffy respectability of the middle class. It stood for freedom of speech and thought and behaviour. It was a rallying-ground for all who disliked the growing Puritan movement – that movement which was destined to triumph, sixty years later, after the Civil War.

There was constant strife between the Puritans and the theatre lovers. The Lord Mayor and his fellow merchants believed in long hours and hard work, thrift, obedience, sobriety, and all the other virtues which made their businesses run smoothly and profitably. They did not want their workmen and apprentices running off to waste their time at plays which might unsettle them and put ideas into their heads.

The city merchants found allies in the preachers, who were prepared to blame every national misfortune on the wickedness of the theatres. Unfortunately for them, the people – masses and nobility alike – loved this form of entertainment. As one preacher sourly lamented: 'Will not a filthy play, with the blast of a trumpet, sooner call thither a thousand, than an hour's tolling of a bell bring to the sermon a hundred?'

The sounding of a trumpet and the hoisting of a flag over the theatre building always signalled that a play was to be performed. The theatres had to be outside the city limits to escape interference from the Lord Mayor, but the people were always willing to come flocking out at the signal.

Fortunately the actors had allies as well as enemies. The Queen, though she did not come to the theatres herself, delighted in 'command performances' in her own palace. Her Master of the Revels arranged these and was constantly co-operating with the theatrical profession. And to checkmate the Puritan attempt to treat actors as 'rogues and vagabonds' each company was protected by some powerful nobleman, such as the Lord High Admiral or the Lord Chamberlain. The company took its name from this patron and in theory the actors were his servants.

Marlowe attached himself to the Admiral's Men, under their brilliant young actor-manager, Edward Alleyn. Shakespeare may have been with them. It was only some years later, when the company had split after a dispute, that we hear of him in the newly formed rival group, the Chamberlain's Men.

These companies were organized like other businesses. The half-dozen or so leading actors were 'sharers', dividing all profits after expenses had been met. Additional characters were played by wage-earning actors, like the journeymen in ordinary trades. Finally there were the usual apprentices, living with the families of the married 'sharers' and taking the women's parts until their voices broke.

Shakespeare made his fortune as a sharer, that is, as an actor and co-manager, not as a dramatist. Companies paid only about five pounds for a new play-script and the author did not receive another penny, however many performances were given. A man could scarcely live by writing plays alone.

At Marlowe's age, however, one did not look too far ahead. Words and ideas were bubbling up in his mind. Very soon he had written his first play, *Tamburlaine the Great*, with a tremendous title role to appeal to Edward Alleyn.

The play told how a Scythian shepherd, 'barbarous and bloody Tamburlaine', rose by a succession of gory stages to the conquest of Central Asia. His first taste of triumph filled him with dreams of world power.

> Is it not passing brave to be a king,
> And ride in triumph through Persepolis?

wrote Marlowe – and proceeded to give his ruthless hero one dazzling triumph after another.

The play was full of the high-pitched ranting and brutal violence in which the Elizabethan theatre audiences delighted. Battle, murder and suicide followed each other at breath-taking speed. The captured Emperor of the Turks was put in a cage until he could stand his ill-treatment no longer and dashed his brains out against the bars, his sympathetic wife following his example a few lines later. It was the sort of stuff the spectators would love, made realistic with genuine blood from the butcher's. When Tamburlaine ordered the captive virgins to be led out and impaled on the lances of his horsemen—

Away with them, I say, and show them Death!

the only drawback was that the execution could not be displayed in action, with 'their slaughtered carcasses' hoisted up on the walls of Damascus.

Not surprisingly, this medley of horrors took the town by storm. Marlowe had to write a sequel, in which Tamburlaine's chariot was drawn on to the stage by kings harnessed like animals and the Governor of Babylon was hung in chains from the walls to be shot at.

Shoot at him all at once [ordered Tamburlaine].
Go now, and bind the burghers hand and foot,
And cast them headlong in the city's lake.
Tartars and Persians shall inhabit there . . .

What may seem more surprising is that Marlowe's play is still remembered as a milestone in the history of English drama.

The reason lies in the quality of the verse. Marlowe had really invented blank verse as we now understand it: the easy-running, five-stress, unrhyming line, which gives the writer maximum freedom and enables the audience to listen to poetry without being reminded of its artificiality. Blank verse is nearest to natural speech, but it gives speech a heightened intensity and beauty. In *Tamburlaine* the new invention is not yet perfected. The stresses sometimes fall too evenly and become monotonous, there are still too many 'end-stopped' lines, where the voice pauses instead of sweeping on. There is still, in *Tamburlaine*, a lot to be done with blank verse to give it the full variety and flexibility of which it is capable. In the next twenty-five years this *was* done, and principally by Shakespeare, taking up the splendid new tool which Marlowe had forged.

For the moment, though, Shakespeare was more occupied with learning his craft as an actor. Marlowe missed all that inside experience. He never had the chance to pick up all the hundred and one scraps of useful knowledge which might have made him, like Shakespeare, a master of stage technique. He remained a poet first and foremost, writing long and splendid speeches for declamation, but weak in construction, characterization, and the other qualities desirable in a play.

How was he living meanwhile?

He did not marry. He showed no interest in women. He had a wide circle of friends, many of them young literary men like himself: Thomas Watson from Oxford, now a law student, a poet and translator; Thomas Nashe from Cambridge, a writer of forceful pamphlets; and Thomas Kyd, who himself soon wrote a notable blank-verse play, *The Spanish Tragedy*. For a time Marlowe shared lodgings with Kyd.

They were a wild lot. In September, 1589, Marlowe and Watson were mixed up in a sword fight in Hog Lane,

Finsbury Fields, which lay between the theatres and the city boundary. Watson killed a man. The jury decided he had done so in self-defence. But Marlowe evidently had a reputation for being quarrelsome. In 1592 a constable and under-constable of Shoreditch asked for protection against him as a dangerous character. Thomas Nashe declared that every writer needed the experience of at least one prison sentence. He gained that experience himself after writing a seditious play entitled *The Isle of Dogs*.

Marlowe had other friends more highly placed in society. He belonged to the intellectual set clustered round Sir Walter Ralegh, a circle believed by its enemies to dabble in black magic, atheism and other wickedness, and referred to sometimes as 'the School of Night'. Probably all its members really did was to discuss questions of interest (including religion) in a freer and more scientific spirit than was usual in the sixteenth century. Mathematicians and astronomers were prominent in the group and Ralegh was keenly interested in chemical experiments. Ralegh, indeed, was interested in most things, including poetry. When Marlowe wrote *The Passionate Shepherd to his Love*, beginning:

Come live with me and be my love . . .

Ralegh retorted with a good-humoured parody in the same metre and the same number of verses.

Marlowe was also friendly with a family named Walsingham. They were relatives of Sir Francis

Walsingham who was, until his death in 1590, the head of the Secret Service. He had raised it to a high pitch of efficiency. He trained his men to break codes, forge documents, and reseal letters so that no one could tell they had been opened. Fifty-three of his agents were planted in key positions all over Europe and he employed a number of other, more shadowy figures, some of them supposed to be working for the other side. Whether Marlowe was ever one of them is among the undisclosed secrets of Walsingham's department.

One thing is sure: Marlowe could not have lived on his earnings as a writer.

Tamburlaine was soon followed by a better play, *The Tragical History of Doctor Faustus*, a treatment of the old German legend of the scholar selling his soul to the Devil.

The power-obsession was still the motif. Faustus, however, wanted more than the political and military domination which had satisfied the Scythian conqueror. Scientific knowledge was the lure, but though Marlowe may have been stimulated by ideas picked up from Ralegh and his friends, Faustus had no use for their leisurely methods of discussion and inquiry. He wanted a short cut to knowledge and the power that went with it. So Marlowe showed him, in a series of flesh-creeping scenes, turning to magic, conjuring up the Devil, and signing a document in his own blood, whereby he sold his soul in return for twenty-four years' service from the fiend.

The rest of the play telescoped those twenty-four years into an hour or two of dramatic action. Faustus had every wish gratified. He could become invisible, he could fly through the world, he could change his shape at will, he could satisfy his curiosity on every subject. If he wanted love, Helen of Troy was brought back to life for him, to be greeted with some of Marlowe's most famous lines:

> Was this the face that launch'd a thousand ships,
> And burnt the topless towers of Ilium? . . .
> O, thou art fairer than the evening air
> Clad in the beauty of a thousand stars.

All too soon the twenty-four years were up, the time of reckoning approached, and a despairing Faustus waited alone in his study for the stroke of midnight and the arrival of the Devil to claim his share of the bargain. Too late he turned to prayer and repentance, begging the stars to stand still in the sky and give him a little grace. Too late.

> The stars move still, time runs, the clock will strike,
> The devil will come, and Faustus must be damn'd.

It was a tremendous last scene which Marlowe wrote for Alleyn. Alone on a bare stage, in broad daylight under the sky, the actor had to build up the atmosphere of the scholar's study at midnight, with his despairing friends praying outside and Hell about to yawn and swallow him. To suggest the suspense and terror of those sixty minutes Alleyn had his acting skill, a clock to strike the half-hours, and some stage thunder and lightning at the end to herald the entrance of the fiends. And he had slightly under sixty lines of Marlowe's magnificent verse.

In the next two or three years Marlowe wrote several other plays. One was *The Jew of Malta*, which may have helped to inspire Shakespeare in his creation of Shylock in *The Merchant of Venice* about five years afterwards. Everybody felt free to borrow ideas from other writers, whether they were contemporaries or ancients. When plays were published in book form – and many were not until after their author's death – it was quite common to omit his name from the title page. What with borrowings and imitations and re-writings and collaborations (not to mention the inclusion of knock-about comedy scenes made up by the actors themselves) it is no wonder that experts, hundreds of years later, cannot be sure exactly who wrote what.

In *Edward the Second* Marlowe turned to English history and wrote a play which is often compared with Shakespeare's tragedy of the other deposed and murdered monarch, *Richard the Second*.

By 1592 not only Marlowe was getting into his stride – other writers were hurrying along the new trail he had blazed. Shakespeare was among them. He had written his earliest and weakest plays (*The Comedy of Errors, Henry the Sixth* and *Titus Andronicus* – the tragedy which rivals Marlowe at his worst and most horrific) and he was being criticized by Robert Greene as an upstart, a mere actor who had not been to a university, who was none the less daring to compete with real writers.

In September of that year all the new playwrights suffered a severe blow. An outbreak of plague closed the London theatres and they did not reopen until June 1594. Alleyn took his company touring in the provinces, but neither they nor the other companies could use any new plays for the time being.

During this period Marlowe himself left the city. He went to stay with the Walsinghams at their country manor at Scadbury, near Chislehurst, in Kent. He was working on *Hero and Leander*, a long narrative poem in rhyme, telling the old Greek story of the two lovers separated by the straits of the Hellespont. It was May 1593. In the quiet of his native Kent, with all the country-side bursting out into the first glories of summer, the twenty-nine-year-old poet wrote vividly and ardently of:

> Hero the fair,
> Whom young Apollo courted for her hair . . .

and

> Amorous Leander, beautiful and young . . .

who used to swim the dangerous narrows at night to visit her in secret.

Marlowe had written only the first part of the story when disaster struck.

On May 12 his former roommate, Kyd, was arrested on suspicion of atheism and sedition: the two things were not easy to separate in Elizabethan England. He broke down under torture and tried to save himself by denouncing Marlowe, declaring that certain incriminating papers were not his but Marlowe's, and had been mixed with his own by accident.

On 18 May the Privy Council issued a warrant for Marlowe's arrest. Two days later the poet appeared before them but was merely told to hold himself available when needed. Scadbury was too far away and London was still full of plague, so he took lodgings near by at Deptford, then a shipbuilding village just down-river. Ten days passed, and still the Privy Council seemed in no hurry to interview him.

On 30 May Marlowe spent most of the day with three other men at a tavern kept by Eleanor Bull in Deptford. The meeting was at the invitation of one of them, Ingram Frizer, who was in Walsingham's service at Scadbury and was thus well acquainted with Marlowe. Frizer, as we now know, had a rather unsavoury record in business matters, but he was outwardly respectable, whereas the second man, Nicholas Skeres, was a common gaol-bird.

The third of Marlowe's companions was Robert Poley, a picturesque and unscrupulous character who had once served as an emissary between Mary Queen of Scots and her friends but had probably worked for the English intelligence service at the same time. He had won – and no doubt betrayed – the confidence of the unhappy conspirator, Anthony Babington. He had served both Sir Philip Sidney and Sir Francis Walsingham. It was probably through the latter that he had first met Marlowe. Apart from his activities as a double spy, Poley had served several stretches of imprisonment in Newgate and the Marshalsea for various offences and he was ripe for any dirty work, from counterfeit coining to stealing a friend's wife.

Strange company, by today's standards! But we must remind ourselves that this was 1593, when famous writers, common criminals and secret agents mixed freely, and when a single person might unite in himself two – or even all three – of those occupations.

What happened that day in Eleanor Bull's tavern at Deptford?

We know that the four men dined at midday, that they strolled in the garden during the afternoon, and that they went back indoors about six o'clock for supper. Their behaviour was quiet and orderly. There was no heavy drinking, no warning signs of a quarrel. But what they were talking about, from ten o'clock in the morning until evening, is something we shall never know.

Suddenly, after supper, there was uproar. Other people rushed into the room. Marlowe was dead or dying, a dagger driven with tremendous force two inches into his brain. It was Frizer's dagger. Frizer himself was bleeding from two superficial cuts about the head. To the excited questioners he declared that there had been a quarrel over paying the bill, Marlowe had attacked him, he had killed Marlowe in self-defence. Poley and Skeres backed up his story.

They repeated it, two days later, to a coroner and six-teen jurymen. Frizer, they said, had been sitting at the table between Poley and Skeres. Marlowe had left the table and was sprawling on a bed behind their backs. He had drawn Frizer's dagger as it dangled from his belt at the rear. Wounded, Frizer had turned, wrested the weapon from him, and struck out in self-defence. He had stabbed Marlowe above the right eye.

There was no one to contradict them. The jurymen viewed the body, measured the wounds, compared them with the dagger. Some may have been puzzled by certain elements in the story. A man, however suddenly enraged, does not usually launch a surprise attack from a reclining position on a bed. Nor does his enemy's head seem the obvious target for a dagger blow from that awkward angle. And why should Frizer, surprised from behind and (according to his story) obstructed by his friends seated on either side of him, escape with trivial flesh wounds? Why should it be his murderous assailant who was disarmed so easily and dispatched with that terrible thrust?

To these problems the jury found no answer. There was not much they could do. Tavern brawls were frequent enough, Marlowe had been in trouble before, he had a peculiar reputation, he was involved even now with the Privy Council. They brought in a verdict that he had been killed by Frizer in self-defence, and in due course a formal pardon was issued which cleared Frizer of responsibility. Long before then, indeed immediately after the inquest finished on 1 June, the poet's body was laid to rest at St Nicholas's, Deptford.

But not the questions. They still tease the minds of re-searching scholars and all whose interest has been stirred by Marlowe's life and character. *Was* this how he died?

Can we accept all the improbabilities? Can we accept the story of three men who (as we now know better than the jurymen did) were all quite untrustworthy and unscrupulous?

Was it really Marlowe who suffered the surprise attack as he lay helpless on the bed?

If so, why? Was it because he was expected any day to give evidence before the Privy Council – and that there was some matter about which he knew too much?

It is unlikely now that we shall ever know.

2. Molière, Master of Comedy

There was deep gloom in the House of the Monkeys – and it was due to more than the December weather in the streets of Paris outside.

The house stood at the corner of the Rue St-Honoré and the Rue des Vieilles Étuves. It owed its name to the splendidly carved pillar which adorned the angle of the building and represented an orange tree with monkeys frisking up and down the trunk. All the district knew it as the House of the Monkeys, but hardly less well known was its occupant, Jean Poquelin, upholsterer by appointment to the King of France. Rich velvets and tapestries, displayed in the front room, proclaimed the nature and quality of his business, while in the attics, above the family's living quarters, the actual work was done which found its way into the noblest châteaux in the kingdom.

The gloom pervading the house on that winter's day in 1642 concerned the future of Jean-Baptiste, Master Poquelin's son. Though now within two or three weeks of his twenty-first birthday, Jean-Baptiste was still far from ceasing to be his father's responsibility, since by the law of France he would not come of age until he was twenty-five.

Jean-Baptiste had recently horrified the family by announcing that he wished to become an actor. The argument had been raging ever since, and the crisis was now at hand.

His father and stepmother had gone over all the objections until they were red in the face, but without avail. It was all right to *go* to the theatre – this was France, thank God, not England, where the Puritans had that very year driven their King from his capital and closed all the playhouses in London. It was even permissible to *write* plays – indeed, no less a personage than Cardinal Richelieu, the real master of France until his death a few weeks before, had condescended to do so and allow them to be produced. But to *act*! That was something very different. A professional actor was beyond the pale. The Church even refused him communion. It was well known that every actor had to renounce his profession formally on his death bed before he could be granted absolution and Christian burial. And it was into this state of permanent sin that Jean-Baptiste Poquelin seemed determined to enter.

It was not even as though he needed the money. Some poor devils, fit for nothing better, might be forgiven if the stage offered the only hope of putting bread into their mouths. Jean-Baptiste had no such excuse. There was the flourishing and respectable business for him to inherit. Was he not the son, grandson and great-grandson of upholsterers? Had not his own mother also (God rest her soul) been the daughter of an upholsterer? And if, despite all this upholstery which was, so to speak, in his blood and the very fabric of his being, the young man wished to turn to some other occupation, had not his father given him every assistance?

The best of educations! Eight years at the Jesuit College of Clermont, where he had rubbed shoulders with young aristocrats like the Prince de Conti and emerged as a first-rate Latin scholar. Then – at his own suggestion, mind! – he had taken his diploma at Orléans and become a qualified lawyer, a procedure which had involved the minimum of study and had been mainly a matter of crossing the right palms with (his father's) silver. So here he was, entitled to practise law or to follow on as royal upholsterer by hereditary appointment, whichever he pleased, and all he wanted to do was become a ragamuffin actor.

It was all, of course, due to 'that woman'.

Madeleine Béjart was the eldest of a large, slightly disreputable theatrical family. Jean-Baptiste had seen and admired her on the stage (for in France, unlike England up to this date, the female characters were played by actresses, not boys) and Master Poquelin had good reason to fear that his son had fallen in love with her. Well he might, for Madeleine was a vivacious, warm-hearted, redheaded young woman with good looks, shrewd wit and free-and-easy ways, not unlike a London actress, Nell Gwyn, who was to captivate Charles the Second a generation later.

Master Poquelin had done his best to rescue his boy from Madeleine's spell. That summer, when it had been part of his duty to join King Louis the Thirteenth campaigning in the south, he had sent young Jean-Baptiste as his deputy. For three months it had been the responsibility of the 'royal upholsterer' to set up and dismantle the King's bedchamber as he moved his headquarters from place to place, a duplicate set of furnishings being provided so that one could always be sent ahead to the next town. From this interesting experience the youth had returned to Paris cured neither of his interest in Madeleine Béjart nor of his insane desire to join her company.

As parental warnings left Jean-Baptiste unmoved, Master Poquelin had played his last card: he had brought in an old friend of the family, a lawyer named Georges Pinel, who had once given the youth private coaching and was liked and respected by him. Perhaps Jean-Baptiste would listen to the unbiased opinion of an outsider? Perhaps fathers were not always the best people to influence their sons?

So, while the one-time tutor and pupil argued behind a closed door, the father and stepmother waited in suspense. After an age Master Pinel and Jean-Baptiste came out, and to everyone's relief they still seemed to be the best of friends. The upholsterer searched his son's face with anxiety – he was not sure of the message in those rather dreamy eyes, but he did not much like the ironical smile playing round the broad lips under the pencil-fine moustache. However, it was for Georges Pinel to announce the result of the conference, so it was to him he put his question. Had he persuaded the boy?

Not exactly. . . . The lawyer cleared his throat with

some embarrassment. It would be truer to say that the boy had persuaded him. . . .

What the devil—? The royal upholsterer nearly burst with indignation. Was the only result of all this long discussion that the young fool was going on the stage after all?

Well, not the *only* result, Master Pinel corrected him. As a matter of fact he, Georges Pinel, had decided to try his luck as an actor himself.

So, about six months later, Pinel and young Poquelin attended a gathering at the house of Madeleine's mother and put their signatures to a document founding a new company to be known as the Illustrious Theatre.

Jean-Baptiste put into it all his own money – that is, his share of what had been left by his dead mother. His father had allowed him to have it, though he was still under age, in return for a paper giving up his hereditary right to follow on as 'royal upholsterer'. This now went to his younger brother.

In return for the capital he put into the company, Jean-Baptiste was to share leading roles with two other actors, turn and turn about. Madeleine was to choose her own parts. Otherwise, the company was to be run on democratic lines, by majority vote. The ten founder members included Madeleine's sister and brother, Geneviève and Joseph – the Béjarts were an extensive family, Madeleine's youngest sister being Armande, still a baby at this time.

It must have been one of the last occasions that Jean-Baptiste signed as 'Poquelin'. Within a year he was using the stage name under which he is immortalized: Molière.

What was the world like, into which he now launched at the age of twenty-one?

The year 1643 was the year in which Louis the Thirteenth was succeeded by his four-year-old son, Louis the Fourteenth. The age of Richelieu – the France depicted so romantically, if not always so realistically, in *The Three Musketeers* – was about to give place to the long reign of 'the Sun King', the creator of Versailles, whose arrogant philosophy was summed up in his own phrase: 'The State? *I* am the State.' This was 'the Great Century' in French history, with Spain declining and England distracted by the quarrels of Cavalier and Roundhead. The political and military successes of France were to be matched with a splendid flowering of literature and the other arts. It was to be her 'Great Century' in the theatre especially, but when Poquelin changed his name to Molière that day had not yet dawned.

The development of the theatre in France and England had followed rather different lines. The French had not got off to the same flying start as the Elizabethans, and their first great dramatist, Pierre Corneille, had appeared in Paris only a few years before this date. The whole approach to play-writing was different. The French were much more anxious to imitate the forms and styles of the ancient Greek and Latin tragedies, while in comedy they were much influenced by the Italian *Commedia dell' Arte,* which involved a great deal of brilliant improvisation on a pre-arranged plot, with the use of stock characters like Harlequin and Pantaloon. So, while the English theatre was still very much the theatre Marlowe had known, until it was banned by the Puritans fifty years after his death, the theatre which Molière was entering at that same moment was based on entirely different models. Also, as we have said, it employed actresses instead of boys. And further, instead of the apron-stage in the London inn yard or open-air theatre, the French performed behind a proscenium arch in an oblong building more like the ordinary public halls we know. A favourite choice was one of those covered tennis courts which played so dramatic a role at the beginning of the French Revolution.

It was in such a tennis court that the Illustrious Theatre opened its first season in the autumn of 1643, and to a second one that it transferred a few months later.

How did Molière take to the strenuous, demanding life into which he had thrown himself with such determination? Was he disappointed in love? Had he hoped to marry the lively Madeleine? We can only speculate around the known facts.

Madeleine was four years older than he – and many more years older in experience of life. She had other loves. For Molière she probably had nothing but liking and affection. Whatever passed between them, they remained good friends and colleagues.

Whether or not he was disappointed in love, Molière was obviously not disappointed in the life of the stage, though he had every excuse for disillusionment. The company did badly. Georges Pinel soon departed, sadder and wiser, and he was not the only one to drop out. Finally, as the unpaid bills mounted, the company went bankrupt. In August, 1645, Molière found himself in prison, held responsible for its debts. He was quickly out again, but there must have been grim pursings of the lips at the House of the Monkeys, and Master Poquelin did not lift a finger to save his son. Let the young idiot learn the hard way! Prison would cure him of his nonsense. He would be glad enough then to quit the stage and return to respectability.

Things did not turn out like that. Molière, Madeleine and their remaining friends did what obstinate actors have always done: having failed to make their mark in the capital, they took to the road and sought success in the provinces. In their case it was a long road. They were to travel it for the next fourteen years.

There were various companies of players touring France in those days, and some of them would have deserved the description as 'rogues and vagabonds' given to such folk in England. This did not apply to Molière and his associates. They linked up with Charles du Fresne, an experienced actor who was well known in the south, and at once acquired a powerful patron in the Duc d'Épernon, viceroy of Guienne. When they were not performing directly as his 'servants' at the splendid Château de Cadillac or some other place of his choice, they were free to range through his spacious province or even beyond its boundaries, using his name as a recommendation and protection.

Molière quickly made an impression on the Duc, who

(we are told) 'held this actor in esteem as a man of wit and intelligence'. Molière was indeed, like most of his colleagues, something else besides an actor. He was – he had to be – a jack-of-all-trades. We know that he was sometimes sent ahead as advance manager, to interview the local councillors, book the hall, and make any other necessary arrangements. No doubt he took his turn in the box office and behind the scenes. All this was useful experience, making him (like Shakespeare but unlike Marlowe) a practical man of the theatre in every sense. Soon he was required to tinker with scripts rather than scenery. Like Shakespeare, he began his writing career by adapting and furbishing up other men's plays. By 1651 he was known as a writer of comedies. But when his first full-length effort was produced at Lyons four years later, a verse-comedy entitled *L' Étourdi* ('The Scatterbrain'), it was still very much a free adaptation of an Italian play, full of stock characters and situations.

By this time the company had lost its first patron and acquired another, that same Prince de Conti who had been at Clermont and was now living in his château at Pézenas, not far from the Mediterranean coast. The Prince, however, though technically an old schoolfellow of Molière's, proved a less reliable friend than the Duc. After some hesitant and rather shabby behaviour he confirmed the engagement of the company, and then some time later, after a serious illness during which he grew worried about the state of his soul, he veered completely round. From being an enthusiast for the theatre, making a fuss over Molière in particular, reading plays with him and discussing every aspect of the drama, he turned against it, denounced the stage and all its works, and went to special pains to dissociate himself from it.

'There are some players here who used to go under my name,' he wrote to the Abbé de Ciron. 'I have taken steps to notify them that they must no longer make use of it and, as you may well believe, I have taken good care not to see them.'

The withdrawal of his favour could no longer do much harm. Molière's company were nearing the end of their long odyssey. They had acted in the castles and town halls and tennis courts of half the kingdom, from Nantes and Bordeaux on the Biscay coast to Grenoble in the shadow of the Alps, from Carcassonne and Avignon in the blazing south to Rouen in the north. They were known as the best company touring the provinces. They were ready for Paris, and to Paris they went the very next year, 1658.

At the House of the Monkeys there was something of a happy family reunion.

The prodigal son had made good. Even Madeleine Béjart was forgiven – after all, Jean-Baptiste had never married her. Indeed, he was still at thirty-six a bachelor, though (as with most stage folk) there was plenty of gossip about the love affairs he was supposed to have carried on with various ladies in the company from time to time. Madeleine, however, remained his friend and business partner, and even the prosperous court upholsterer had to admit that her pretty red head contained a good deal of practical ability. She and Molière were the organizing brains of the company. While he explored the possibilities of finding a noble patron, she negotiated for premises to perform in. As the Béjarts no longer had a family home in Paris, Master Poquelin allowed her to give the House of the Monkeys as her address.

Molière found the required patron in no less a person than the King's younger brother. Louis himself was still only twenty, chafing under the control of the Queen Mother, Anne of Austria, and his chief Minister, Cardinal Mazarin. Until he married and had a son, the heir to the throne would be this brother, always known by the title of 'Monsieur'. For this reason Molière's company now styled themselves *La Troupe de Monsieur*.

They made their first appearance in the vast guard room of the old Louvre palace on October 24, 1658. Cromwell had died a month before: if there were any aristocratic English exiles among the courtiers that evening, they were probably counting the days until such festivities would be possible again in their own country. For Molière and his friends also it was an evening for the anxious assessment of their chances. Not only was the King out there in front but so were his own royal players from the Hôtel de Bourgogne, where there was no performance that night. Unchallenged as the foremost tragic actors in France, they were of all people the most qualified to criticize and least likely to show mercy to the newcomers.

It was unfortunate, but perhaps inevitable, that the main item on the programme was a tragedy by Corneille, *Nicomède*. The royal players had a reputation for Corneille, they produced each of his plays as it was written, everyone at court had already seen what they could do with this one. But Monsieur's company would scarcely have considered making their début in comedy. Tragedy was more highly regarded, comedy was somehow inferior. Molière himself still cherished dreams of shining in the higher form of drama, and even if he personally would have preferred something lighter on this occasion, he had only his one vote to cast against those of Madeleine and the rest. So they played the tragedy, adequately but without brilliance. There was polite applause but no more. Probably the royal actors, at least, clapped more loudly than they would have done had the performance been better. Clearly these newcomers were not going to be serious rivals.

Then, to the surprise of some (for the practice of curtain speeches was going out of fashion in Paris), Molière came downstage, bowed low to the King, and began to express the thanks of his company. It was a modest speech, with a graceful compliment for the King's own actors, those 'excellent originals' of which he and his friends represented only 'feeble copies'.

'But now,' he concluded, 'since Your Majesty has been so good as to put up with our country ways, I beg most humbly for permission to present one of those little trifles which have won me a certain reputation and with which I have been in the habit of amusing the provinces.'

Molière retired amid kindly applause. In a few moments he reappeared in the title part of *The Amorous Doctor*, a comedy sketch he had written and often played on tour. Now he was in his element. The hard school of

the provinces had taught him how to get the maximum
effect from every lift of his left eyebrow, every twinkle of
his dark eyes, every expressive change in his mobile
features. And, though the script of *The Amorous Doctor*
has long vanished, we may believe that he had good
material to work on. As a kindly but acute observer of
mankind in all its absurdity, Molière had by now
gathered the bricks and mortar for that great edifice of
comedy which is his contribution to French literature.

The King laughed heartily and continually. When a
king laughs, others are quick to see the joke. *The Amorous
Doctor* saved the evening. Even the royal players agreed
that, when it came to broad comedy, these provincials
compared very favourably with the Italian troupe established in the hall of the Petit Bourbon on the south side of
the rambling old palace. And sure enough, a day or two
later, came word from the King that *La Troupe de Monsieur* was to share this hall on alternate evenings with the
Italian comedians.

Madeleine was able to cancel her separate arrangements
for hiring the Marais tennis court. They were 'in'.

The Petit Bourbon was an elegant hall, its sides lined
with Doric columns, its vaulted ceiling adorned with
painted lilies. The Italians had been at some pains to adapt
it as a theatre, so it was agreed quite amicably that
Molière's company should make a contribution towards
this expense and that the Italians should play on the three
best nights of the week, Tuesday, Friday and Sunday,
while the newcomers occupied the stage on the other four,

less popular, evenings. The two companies were quite friendly. The Italians were comedians, whereas Molière's colleagues insisted on starting with a series of Corneille's tragedies, which were not very well received. The Italian company was headed by a renowned *Commedia dell' Arte* actor, Tiberio Fiorillo, better known as 'Scaramouche', the name of the stock character he played. Later, Molière's enemies accused him of copying Scaramouche, but in fact the Italian was a clown of genius, with the coarse humour that went out of fashion as French society became more and more refined, and Molière's entirely different 'comedy of manners', polished, witty and delicate, was the style which took its place.

True, in the past, Molière had never been too proud to learn from the Italian theatre. Long ago he had written *Scatterbrain*, based on Italian models. Now, when the Corneille tragedies did not bring in the Parisian public (who preferred to see them better done elsewhere), he put on *Scatterbrain* and another of his early Italian-style comedies. Again, as at the opening performance before the King, the response was enthusiastic. As even one of his jealous enemies was compelled to record, 'It was nothing but "ha ha!" throughout the audience!' In the spring His Majesty came back to Paris after an absence and attended five performances. In June Scaramouche went off to his native Italy and the *Troupe de Monsieur* was able to use the theatre every night of the week. Thus, without neglecting tragedy, they had scope for more comedy. About the same time their veteran leader, Charles du Fresne, retired from the stage, and there were other changes in the company which strengthened Molière's power and gave him more chance to develop his special gifts. This was the year, 1659, in which he wrote *Les Précieuses Ridicules*, and what we call the comedy of manners was born.

A neat translation of the title is difficult. A *précieuse* was one of those intellectual women who had lately made their appearance in upper-class society and who in England, a century later, were termed 'blue-stockings'. They included women like Madame de Sévigné, one of the world's finest letter writers, and they represented a step towards sex equality, for they showed that women could hold their own with men in the discussion of literature, art, and public affairs. Their drawing-room parties, or *salons*, were a civilizing element, teaching people the good manners of conversation and the much-needed art of courteous disagreement rather than angry argument. The *salons* of France started a tradition which spread to other countries and survived into the twentieth century – when its disappearance left a social gap still lamented by many.

Molière had no wish to make fun of the truly clever woman – but he was amused, now he was living in Paris again, to see how the new fashion had produced its imitators. There was a type of woman (she still exists, and *her* disappearance would be less of a disaster) who pretended an interest she did not really feel; who was ready to chatter glibly about the latest book but not so ready to sit down and read it; and who was always in ecstasies about some new intellectual fashion without having any

ANNO DÑI ÆTATIS SVÆ 21
1585

OD ME NVTRIT
E DESTRVIT

Portrait of a young man thought by
some to be Marlowe

Jean-Baptiste Molière

solid knowledge on which to form an opinion. These pretentious, affected ladies were the *précieuses ridicules* against whom he directed his satire. Though the type is universal (its modern representatives culling their 'talking-points' from glossy magazines and Sunday newspapers), the Parisian *salons* of this date had produced a particularly absurd and exaggerated variety. The common-sense rules of decent speech and behaviour had been refined into an artificial code of conventions, and in their desperate efforts to make an impression the *précieuses* wrapped up their meagre thoughts in more and more obscure and high-flown language. The one simple word in constant use was 'darling', with which everybody addressed everybody else.

This was the blown-up cult which Molière punctured with his one-act comedy. Its first performance rocked the audience with wave after wave of laughter. Everyone knew the type so well. Even the *précieuses* themselves had to laugh as convincingly as they could – they had never dared to be in a minority before and dared not start now. Also they hoped by their smiles to suggest that the satire could not possibly be aimed at themselves. Would they fight back in secret? That question must have been in many minds, including the author's, and it was to hearten him that one delighted gentleman rose in the audience and shouted: 'Stick to it, Molière! This is good comedy!' Further performances were held up for two weeks while a copy of the script was sent post-haste to the King, who was away in the Pyrenees. Louis liked the play. There was no further hope of suppressing it. It was acted again, with doubled prices. There were forty-four performances in the first year, including several by royal command. With one great gust of laughter Molière had destroyed a whole ridiculous fashion and rid the *salons* of their worst silliness.

He had done something more. He had found his true vocation as a satirist of human folly in general and of French society in particular. 'No longer need I take Plautus and Terence as my models,' he said. 'I have only to study the world.'

Paris knew him now as a playwright, but he was still, and all his life, the hard-working actor-manager with all the cares which such a position brings. A heavy blow fell in 1660 when, without any warning to the players, the Office of Works demolished their theatre. Luckily they had now not only the patronage of Monsieur but the warm friendship of his brother, the King. Louis promised them a new theatre in the Palais Royal near by. Until it was ready they were to act before him in the Louvre and in the houses of the nobility. After a few months the company were able to open in their new home, and in one way at least the removal proved a good thing: at the Petit Bourbon they had been tied to the Italians' permanent single set, representing a public street with various houses opening out upon it, and this often gave their own plays an air of unreality, when confidential discussions had to take place on doorsteps which in normal life would have been carried on inside. At the Palais Royal the company were free to make a fresh start with removable scenery and Molière could write his future plays with as many changes of set as were required.

Not only future plays, but his own future life, now occupied his thoughts. He would soon be forty and he did not propose to remain a bachelor much longer. He persuaded his fellow shareholders to grant him a second share in the profits if he should marry. They could hardly have refused, for they must have realized by now how much their success depended upon him. Madeleine Béjart, still the other dominant member of the company, would certainly not have voted against him, for the bride he had in mind was her own youngest sister, Armande.

Armande was, indeed, young enough to be her daughter. She was only eighteen or nineteen – twenty-four years separated the eldest and the youngest of the innumerable Béjarts – and perhaps her greatest attraction for Molière was that she reminded him of the beautiful and lively red-headed Madeleine he had known when he first became an actor. He had watched Armande grow up. He had been content to wait until she was old enough to know her own mind.

Molière, with his deep and compassionate knowledge of human nature, was well aware of the problems threatening a marriage between a young girl and a middle-aged man. That same year he wrote *The School for Husbands*, in which two elderly brothers plan to marry their pretty young wards. One man believes in strict methods. A woman's place is in the home, mending and knitting, and that is where he will keep his wife, nor shall she 'ever stir outside without someone to keep an eye on her'. His brother, Aristo, is much more broad-minded. Young women, he says, 'love to enjoy a little freedom. Suspicious precautions, bolts and bars, make neither wives nor maidens virtuous.' This was closer to Molière's opinion, but in the play he took the part of the smug and pompous Sganarel, who thinks his easy-going brother is a fool but is himself the one to be fooled in the end.

Among those who enjoyed *The School for Husbands* was Monsieur's new bride, the Princess Henrietta of England, better known as Minette, Charles the Second's beloved sister. She and her husband saw it, with her royal brother-in-law, at the Château of Vaux, where Louis's minister, Fouquet, put on one of those lavish entertainments so typical of the period. The grounds, with their twelve hundred sparkling fountains, foreshadowed the glories of Versailles itself, soon to be created by the same landscape artist. Eighty tables were set out for the host of banqueters with six or seven thousand pieces of gold plate. Fouquet himself was on his way down – his disgrace and arrest followed shortly afterwards – but Molière, as the playwright and actor-manager commissioned to contribute to such an occasion, was emphatically on his way up. He had the King's favour. In the years to come he was to arrange many more such gala performances at Versailles itself.

Early in the next year there was a family conference at the house which the Béjarts now occupied in the Place du Palais Royal, close to the theatre. Molière's father and brother-in-law were there to support him. Old Madame

Béjart did the honours, but Madeleine, as always, was the real spokesman of her clan. It was for her, probably, a most happy occasion. She had been Molière's friend and colleague for the best part of twenty years. Now he was to marry Armande, the 'baby' of the family and for a long time the pet of the whole company. Armande was pretty and vivacious, with promise as an actress and an individual taste in dress, always striking in appearance but no slavish follower of fashion. Molière would have a charming bride, but Armande was no less lucky in her husband. Molière was a good man and he was in a prosperous position. No elder sister could have wished for a better match.

So the marriage contract was read and signed according to the serious tradition of French family life, and a few weeks later, on Shrove Tuesday, the wedding took place. In due time the first of their several children was born and the King himself stood godfather by proxy.

The years which now followed were busy ones for Molière. *The School for Husbands* led to his writing *The School for Wives,* and criticisms of this play led in turn to a witty retort in *The School for Wives Criticized.* Armande made her real début in this piece and showed herself a comic actress of considerable ability. In the space of a single decade Molière enriched the world's drama with a succession of unforgettable comedies – *Tartuffe, Le Misanthrope, L'Avare* ('The Miser'), *Le Médecin Malgré Lui* ('The Mock Doctor'), *Le Malade Imaginaire* ('The Health Faddist'), *Le Bourgeois Gentilhomme* ('The

Self-made Gentleman'), and others. Besides writing, producing and acting in these, he had to waste a good deal of his time on arranging the spectacular entertainments which also appealed to Louis. He had, for example, to organize a six-day programme for Versailles, entitled *The Pleasures of the Enchanted Isle*, and as these shows involved music, ballet, elaborate scenery and effects (as well as the harmonious dovetailing of innumerable separate items) the mind boggles at the thought of the burden he had to bear. Yet somehow he had to make time to write his own contribution to the festivities.

This was the price to be paid for being the King's favourite entertainer. And he needed the King's favour. He was surrounded by jealous enemies. Each new comedy stung someone with its satire. The royal actors hated him for toppling them off their pedestal as leaders of the profession. Molière's private life and character, as well as his ideas, were assailed on every side with slanders and libels. Armande did not help him. She was young and inexperienced, with few of her elder sister's mental qualities. The pretty face might recall Madeleine's twenty years before, but there was not, and never would be, anything like Madeleine's brain behind it. Armande was a spoilt child. She behaved and spoke as she pleased, never pausing to wonder whether she was causing embarrassment to her husband and offering a handle to his enemies.

Nothing, though, could have won him half as much enmity as one of his own plays, *Tartuffe*.

This was a scathing satire on religious hypocrites. Tartuffe is an unscrupulous impostor who worms his way into a pious family, deceives them into thinking him almost a saint, and proceeds to misuse their trust in every way. Tartuffe, with his mock humility, his pretence of devoutness, and his glib Church patter, personifies all the things which have done most harm to true Christianity since it was founded. In writing the play Molière was attacking not religion but humbug. Unfortunately real life is full of people who, like the characters in his comedy, find it hard to tell the difference. Long before *Tartuffe* was acted – when, indeed, it was still only a script to which the author was known to be putting the final touches – the opposition began to mobilize.

There had been for years a kind of secret society, the Company of the Holy Sacrament, including reformed aristocrats like Molière's one-time friend and patron, the Prince de Conti, who formed what we should nowadays call a 'pressure group' or 'lobby' to exert what they considered to be the right moral influence in governing circles. On April 17, 1664, they held a meeting at which each member promised to do his utmost, by speaking to everyone he knew at court, to block production of 'the wicked comedy of *Tartuffe*', though at this date they could not have read the play and knew only its general idea.

Two weeks later Molière went to Versailles, taking the manuscript with him. He read it to Louis, who much enjoyed it and had it performed for his courtiers. The opposition then went into the attack. The Archbishop of Paris, once the King's tutor, set to work on his former pupil. Louis, while publicly admitting that he had found the comedy 'extremely diverting' and 'did not doubt the good intentions of the author', was induced to agree that simpler folk might not take the satire in the way it was intended, and with reluctance he banned it from public performance. Even this did not satisfy the author's most virulent opponents. The vicar of St Barthélemy published a pamphlet suggesting that Molière 'should be burned at the stake as a foretaste of the fires of Hell'. This was going much too far, and the vicar was given a stiff reprimand from the King he had just gone out of his way to flatter.

Molière, for all his genial good humour, was a fighter when it came to a matter of principle. He was not going to be silenced by the opposition. He needed *Tartuffe* for his next season at the Palais Royal. Apart from the inconvenience and financial loss caused by the ban, his reputation was at stake. He hurried to and fro between Paris and Versailles, trying to get the ban taken off. He pointed out that, until the play had been publicly acted so that people could form their own opinion, he was like a man condemned without trial. He suggested very tactfully that the King would lose dignity if the situation remained unaltered. Having approved the play originally, he was being made to look as though he had changed his mind under pressure – as though he, the Sun King, had not sufficient faith in his own literary judgement. Louis was embarrassed but dared not take off the ban. But he was otherwise loyal to his favourite playwright, and in the following year, when Molière had raised a storm with another play, he made a grand gesture which nobody could misunderstand: he asked his brother to give up the patronage of Molière's company to himself, and henceforth they were known as *La Troupe du Roi*.

It happened now as usually happens when a work of literature is suppressed by censorship: nobody could rest until he had read *Tartuffe* and found out what it was all about. Molière did not dare to let it out of his possession. Had he done so he would probably have lost the copyright, which he reckoned was worth twenty thousand crowns to himself and his company if ever they were allowed to act the play. *Tartuffe* was discussed all over Europe. Queen Christina of Sweden told her librarian to write to the French foreign minister, requesting a copy – but even she had to be refused. Molière was pursued by society hostesses begging him to give private readings to their guests at evening parties. There was no ban on this, or even on private performances, and he was glad to use every opportunity to marshal support on his side. He felt sure that most people, if only they could hear the play for themselves, would agree that there was nothing objectionable in it.

The King helped him. He arranged a private reading at Fontainebleau for the papal legate and his suite: the Italian cardinal thoroughly enjoyed it. And when Monsieur, while still the company's patron, commanded a private performance, Louis not only attended it but brought his wife and mother.

Molière meanwhile revised the play, changing its title to *The Impostor* and doing everything he could to remove causes for misunderstanding and offence, without abandoning the essential purpose of his satire. At last, three years after all the trouble had started, the King yielded and removed the ban, after which he departed to take command of his army in Flanders and cause the usual embarrassment to his professional generals. Perhaps he felt it would be quieter at the front than in Paris when the comedy at last achieved public performance.

If so, he was not far wrong. *Tartuffe* – or *The Impostor* – was presented on a Friday, with eager theatre-goers storming the building as though it were a fortress. The next performance was announced for the Sunday, but on Saturday soldiers arrived to tear down the playbills and to picket the entrance. The play was banned again by authority of Lamoignan, President of Parliament, who exercised special extra powers during the absence of His Majesty at the wars. Molière hurried to see him and protest. He might have saved his breath if he had known that Lamoignan was a member of the secret society sworn to keep *Tartuffe* off the stage. Lamoignan received him with a suave hypocrisy which would not have been out of place in the comedy. He admitted that the play was 'a fine and instructive piece of work', but added: 'The theatre is no place for preaching the gospel.' Then he cut short the interview, saying he had to go to a church service.

Lamoignan had really overruled the King: surely, thought Molière, the King would now overrule Lamoignan? On the Monday two trusted members of the company set off post-haste to find Louis at his headquarters. By Thursday the secret society had played its next card: the Archbishop of Paris came out with a threat of excommunication against anyone concerned not merely with a public showing of *Tartuffe* but with even a private recital in any form. Louis was meantime assuring the actors that all would be well, that he would look into the matter the moment he returned, and that the comedy would definitely be licensed. The Archbishop's announcement came as a bombshell. Even His Majesty was shaken. When he came back from the campaign a month later he found the theatre still shut. It stayed shut for seven weeks in all – and when it reopened it was not with *Tartuffe*. Excommunication was something Louis could not face.

Censors seldom win the last battle of all. Molière fought on. After a year the ban was cautiously tested by a private performance at Chantilly. Nothing happened. A few months later Louis judged it safe to license the play in its second, revised form. Four days afterwards it was staged in public – and for twenty-eight consecutive performances, with another twenty in the course of the year: remarkable figures for that period. Printed copies, at a crown apiece, were sold out within a week of publication.

What did Armande make of this wearisome struggle? Most likely she was puzzled and impatient that her husband should make such a fuss about one play. It would have been so much simpler to write another, so much wiser to keep out of quarrels with important people and to entertain the public without shocking anybody. Armande was no doubt surprised and delighted when at last the ban was broken and the money came rolling in, but she had little real understanding of Molière's purpose and achievement. In the simplest terms it was this: he had come into a theatre in which only tragedy was admired and considered as possessing literary value, and by his efforts he had raised comedy to the same level. Before his time it had been a coarse, knock-about, unsubtle medium. He had demonstrated that it could be used to show men the truth about themselves, their neighbours, and the whole of human society.

Armande, never troubled by too much intellect, was no partner for such a man. She was young and frivolous. The gentlemen of fashion flocked round her, paying compliments and flirting. After trekking round the dusty provinces throughout her childhood and teens, Armande revelled in the gaieties of Paris and Versailles. Few middle-aged husbands could have kept up with her – and Molière was not only middle-aged but overworked and unwell. He was writing, acting, producing, for ever at the beck and call of the King. Living on a milk diet himself, he had to scurry through a world of banqueting noblemen and hard-drinking theatre folk without ever losing his characteristic sweetness of temper.

With Armande there *were* quarrels, though they were kept quiet and he was too loyal ever to discuss his unhappy home life even with his closest friends.

One quarrel arose out of his kindness to a twelve-year-old boy actor, Michel Baron, an orphan who was being exploited by a third-rate company. Molière was impressed by the child's talent and horrified by the way he was being treated. He got an order from the King to take over custody of the orphan and proceeded to adopt him, though the actress from whom Baron had been rescued came storming round to Molière's house with a brace of pistols in her hands. It was Armande, however, who caused the most trouble. She was jealous of her husband's interest in this outsider and when they began rehearsals together she flew into a tantrum and boxed the boy's ears. Baron ran to the King, asked leave to resign his part, and went back to his old exploiter for another three or four years' hard labour in the provinces. There was a happy ending to the story. When Molière learnt how much the youth was regretting his action, he obtained a royal order authorizing his return to the company and sent it to him with a kindly letter inviting him to come back. Baron arrived travel-stained, penniless, and speechless with gratitude. In later years he became the leading actor in the newly founded Comédie Française and indeed one of the greatest actors in the annals of the French theatre. Molière's judgement had been good.

Meanwhile, Molière and Armande agreed to separate, at least for a time. His health made it advisable for him to live at Auteuil, near the Bois de Boulogne, not a suburb then but a country village popular with literary men. Armande could not live without the pleasures of the city and she was not the sort of wife to sacrifice herself. They continued to work together at the theatre, but they knew that otherwise they were better apart. However, after four years they tried again. Molière gave up his tiresome diet and ate meat again, but his health suffered. They had another son, but he died at the age of three weeks. They had lost their first boy, the King's godson, at a year old and now had only a daughter aged five.

Another sorrow, earlier in that same year, 1672, was the death of Madeleine Béjart.

On the anniversary of that day, 17 February, in the following year, Molière was playing the lead in *Le Malade Imaginaire*, a play he had recently completed and in which, with his usual sense of humour, he had managed to laugh at those who worried too much about their health. That night he felt like death. Even Armande was concerned about his appearance and joined with Baron in urging him not to go on. But Molière, labouring under a chill and racked by his cough, thought only of his company.

'What am I to do?' he demanded. 'We have fifty poor work people on our books, paid by the day. What happens to them if we cancel the performance? I should never forgive myself.'

Somehow, with great difficulty, he got through the play. There was a tragic irony in the whole situation. He, with the hand of death upon him, was pretending to be a healthy man fussing over imaginary ailments. His actor's technique never deserted him. He had the audience almost hysterical with amusement. Even when, in the final fantastic scene, he was gripped by a terrible convulsion, he managed to cover it by forcing a laugh.

In the dressing room Baron asked anxiously how he felt. 'Cold,' said Molière. 'I am cold. Fit to die of it.' Baron got him a sedan chair and walked beside it to the playwright's house in the Rue de Richelieu. Two Sisters of Charity were staying there as guests. They helped to get him to bed. Armande went off to fetch a pillow stuffed with herbs, which was supposed to promote sound sleep. Molière had a violent fit of coughing and spat blood. Baron exclaimed at the sight of it. 'No need to be frightened,' gasped Molière. 'All the same, go and ask my wife to come.' When Baron and Armande came hurrying back a few moments later he was dead.

He had previously begged for a priest. Two had refused to come. The third, dragged from his bed, arrived too late. As a result it was possible for the authorities to refuse his body Christian burial. Armande, championing her dead husband as she had never done in his lifetime, went storming indignantly to the King. 'They refuse a tomb,' she declared, 'to the man who deserves an altar.' In the end the Archbishop grudgingly gave permission for the funeral 'on condition that there shall be no ceremony, with two priests only, after nightfall, and no solemn service in any church'. These instructions were not strictly enforced – Molière had too many loyal friends to allow him to be thrust underground in this furtive fashion – but the vindictiveness of his enemies denied him the honour he had so well deserved. Like Mozart a century later, the prince of comic writers who had so much enriched the theatres of the world was left to lie in an unmarked grave.

3. The Incomparable Siddons

It was an evening in the early seventeen-seventies. Young King George the Third was on the throne of England and the stupidity of his ministers was gradually pushing the American colonists towards the revolution which was to burst out a few years later. It was no such high political matter, however, which had produced the atmosphere of tension among the audience in the little Welsh town of Brecon.

There was something special about tonight's performance. It was the farewell 'benefit' for Mr William Siddons, who was leaving Mr Kemble's Company of Comedians. This would not, in itself, have caused much stir. Mr Siddons, though a good-looking and well-set-up young man of twenty-eight, was no great shakes as an actor. Even by the modest standards of the Kemble company he was no more than adequate. No, as more than one lady whispered to her neighbour behind her fan, it was the circumstances of his sudden departure which were interesting. One might guess at a good deal of drama taking place behind the scenes, which the tantalized audience would not be privileged to hear.

Mr Siddons was in love with Miss Kemble, the

Sarah Siddons: from a portrait by Lawrence in
the Tate Gallery

Giuseppe Verdi

manager's eldest daughter – the seventeen-year-old Sarah, dark-eyed and black-haired, attractive and as refined off-stage as she was talented when acting. Brecon took a special interest in Sarah. Had she not been born in the town, at the Shoulder of Mutton Inn, during one of the company's earlier visits on July 5, 1755? Brecon had watched her grow up, year by year, and noted her development each time the Kembles' touring programme brought them back.

Brecon knew her parents, too, and knew that they had dreams of a better husband for Sarah than this young man was likely to make.

The amusing thing was that history seemed to be repeating itself. Mrs Kemble had been the daughter of an actor-manager, Mr Kemble had been a member of her father's company, and *her* parents had had very different ideas for her. When the marriage had gone through despite their opposition, her father had tried to save his dignity by pretending (unfairly in this case) that Roger Kemble was no actor and never would be. He had forbidden his daughter to marry an actor, yes, but as Roger was not one, she had not really disobeyed him. This feeble excuse was soon shown to be nonsense when his son-in-law and daughter took over the company and continued to operate it successfully throughout the West Midlands and the Marches of Wales.

But – *would* history repeat itself?

Would the formidable Mrs Kemble, now the mother of twelve, allow the lovesick Sarah to get round her as easily as she had got round her own parents?

Apparently not. Mrs Kemble had far more suitable young men lined up for her daughter. All Brecon knew about the local squire, Mr Evans, who had fallen desperately in love with her after hearing her sing "Robin, Sweet Robin." And there were half a dozen other young gentlemen interested. The Kembles covered a lot of ground in their tours – in the course of a year their wagon of scenery and properties might rumble from Lancashire to the Bristol Channel, and as far east as Warwickshire – and Sarah's attractions were widely noticed.

Since the company arrived back in Brecon, things had come to a head. Mr Siddons, alarmed by the competition of Mr Evans, with his landed estate and impressive income, had begged Sarah to elope with him. The girl had very properly refused to deceive her parents. Elopements were all right in plays but not in real life. Mr Siddons had made an angry scene with Mr and Mrs Kemble. They had dismissed him. To avoid more trouble than had already been caused, it was agreed that he should leave with the usual benefit performance accorded to actors departing in more harmonious circumstances.

There could be very few, if any, of the audience who were not well aware of all this, for in a small and normally quiet market town like Brecon any gossip was welcome and travelled fast. So, as they settled themselves in their seats for a mediocre performance of a mediocre play, they could look forward to the extra titillation of seeing at close quarters most of the characters (but not Mr Evans) who were taking part in the parallel drama proceeding behind the scenes. Stage dialogue took on a double meaning.

Every glance and gesture was watched for an indication of the secret emotions mingling with those appropriate to the play. As the Kemble Company was very much a family affair, with Sarah's young brothers and sisters cast wherever possible to save the wages of outsiders, the audience that evening felt sure of getting their money's worth.

They did. When the performance ended, Mr Siddons advanced alone to the footlights and prepared to acknowledge the applause in the usual speech of thanks and farewell. No one was surprised when this speech proved to be in rhymed verse – that sort of epilogue was quite common. What sent a delicious shiver down the spines of the audience was the realization that this clumsy effusion was the young actor's own composition, that he had entitled it "The Discarded Lover," and that its eleven verses were devoted to his shameful treatment by the Kembles. Having delivered it with feeling (and perhaps with more dramatic effect than he ever achieved in all his other stage appearances put together), Mr Siddons bowed and retired into the wings – where the infuriated Mrs Kemble was lurking in ambush and boxed his ears so resoundingly that only the continued applause prevented the audience's hearing.

So ended an eventful evening. But things could never be quite the same again. William Siddons might be cast into the outer darkness, but Sarah was more in love with him than ever, and was not to be comforted with Mr Evans or any other substitute.

Mrs Kemble could not lock up her daughter. She did

the next best thing. Sarah was found a post as lady's maid and companion to Lady Mary Greatheed, who lived in a secluded country mansion in Warwickshire. There, surely, nothing much could happen to a rebellious seventeen-year-old.

Guy's Cliff is even today a favourite beauty spot. In 1771, with its peace and privacy still unbroken, it was doubly romantic and suitably melancholy for the nursing of a broken heart.

The house itself was elegant and modern. It had been largely rebuilt, about twenty years before, on the basis of a much older dwelling which had developed out of a medieval chapel. It stood on a rocky bluff, clothed in tall trees. The courtyard was a dell, walled on three sides by the cliff, in whose face artificial caves had been hewn for stables. Below the house spread a mirror-like expanse of river, broadened out into a great quiet pool after it had come frothing past a water mill first mentioned in Domesday. The river was the Avon. From Guy's Cliff it flowed on past the massive walls of Warwick Castle and then, after a few more miles, past the resting place of Shakespeare in Stratford parish church.

However romantic and melancholy this setting, with its mossy rocks and shadowy caves, its murmurous waters and whispering trees, it was not a sad house. True, Lady Mary was a widow, but she was not old – the son and heir, Bertie, was only eleven – and she was a kind mistress, with a sense of humour. Herself the daughter of the Duke of Ancaster, she confessed in later years that she always felt an impulse to stand up when Sarah entered the room, for the girl already had so much presence and natural dignity.

Sarah needed it. Her father's occupation put her in an awkward, intermediate position in the class-conscious eighteenth century. She was neither a lady nor a menial.

She had come up against snobbery in her earliest years. The Kembles had been anxious for her to have the best education possible in the difficult circumstances of their wandering life, and they had sent her to several different private schools as opportunity offered. She had spent most time at Thornlea House in Worcester – and there was nothing to equal an old-fashioned cathedral city for grading the children according to whether their fathers were clergy, gentry, professional, or 'in trade'. The daughter of a touring actor ranked low indeed, and for a long time the other girls had been chilly and superior, until they suddenly realized what a tremendous asset Sarah Kemble could be in the production of school plays. After that, she had been popular enough.

Even at that age, she had been used to acting in public. Schoolwork had to be set aside whenever her services were needed for her father's productions. It was at Worcester, when she was twelve, that she first found herself acting with William Siddons. The play had been *Charles the First*. She had been cast as Princess Elizabeth, William as the Duke of Richmond. There had been countless other appearances as the company wove its way up and down the West Midlands, playing sometimes in the expanding industrial centres like Birmingham and Wolverhampton, sometimes in the sheep-market towns of the Border, like Kington and Leominster.

So, at seventeen, Sarah was an accomplished young woman. Her elocution was exceptional, her singing voice true and pleasant. She played the harpsichord, she had a good taste for poetry, she had the prodigious memory of the born repertory actress, and her deportment (to judge from its effect upon her aristocratic mistress) fitted her for the best society in the land.

Sarah's duties probably included reading aloud, but her full talents were appreciated only when Lady Mary took her on a visit to the Duchess of Ancaster in Lincolnshire. Sarah took her meals in the servants' hall, though her status gave her a good position among the senior staff such as the butler and cook. Here, as at school, her stage experience won her sudden popularity. She was able to entertain her companions with dramatic recitations, a treat which can be imagined only if one remembers the isolation of a country mansion in those days and the scarcity of other amusements, especially for working people. The rumour of these electrifying performances 'below stairs' reached the ears of Lady Mary's brother, Lord Robert Bertie, and he went to the servants' hall to hear for himself. He was vastly impressed and told the rest of the family. Lady Mary told him he must not encourage the girl too much. Her parents did not want their children to follow in their own arduous and uncertain profession. They were apprenticing two of her sisters as a milliner and a dressmaker respectively, and they were sending her brother, John Philip, to train for the Roman Catholic priesthood at Douai, the English College in France. Lord Robert must not give Sarah ideas of going on the stage. Poetry was safe enough. Lady Mary herself gave Sarah a copy of Milton, knowing that Milton was her favourite author.

Meantime, the schemes of Mr and Mrs Kemble were being upset in another way. Sarah was still in correspondence with William Siddons, and even seeing him when his travels brought him within reach of Guy's Cliff.

They were determined to get married. The Kembles at last gave in. They could scarcely have forgotten how they themselves had battled against parental opposition. In the autumn of 1773 Sarah left Guy's Cliff – though not for ever, for she was destined to return in after years as an honoured guest of the family she had once served.

On November 25, still only eighteen, she married William in the ancient church of Holy Trinity at Coventry. Her father gave her away. All was (more or less) forgiven. Sarah returned to the bosom of her family and the company, bringing William back with her. There was no question now of not going on the stage. They had to eat. There was nothing William could do but act, and that not very well, so the bride too must work.

Within two or three weeks the immortal name of 'Sarah Siddons' made its first appearance on the playbills.

What was life like on the English stage in 1773 – that life from which the Kembles tried to save their children but which they showed no signs of quitting themselves?

How did it differ from that of Marlowe's time, nearly two centuries before?

The touring companies still played where they could, in barns, halls, inn yards, and wherever the local authorities did not forbid them. They were still liable to be treated as rogues and vagabonds, but sometimes they were made welcome and allowed to play in market halls and other public buildings, patronized by the mayor and the leading citizens. The atmosphere varied from town to town. Whereas the Elizabethan actors had been up against the Puritans, their eighteenth-century successors had to contend with the new movement called Methodism.

In the bigger provincial centres, however, there was now a permanent playhouse, usually called the Theatre Royal after the famous one first established in Drury Lane in 1663, when the return of Charles the Second brought a resurrection of the drama in England. But (as the name suggests) a new theatre could only be established by royal permission, obtained through the Lord Chamberlain. This official had also, since 1737, wielded absolute authority over all new scripts, and no new play could be presented without his licence. This censorship was originally applied for political reasons, but in the course of generations it was to be extended to cover a bewildering and often illogical selection of taboos.

The theatre building itself was very different from those run by Burbage and Alleyn and was more like those used by Molière. The acting area had receded behind the picture frame of the proscenium arch and, although the 'quality' might still sit to left and right, at ninety degrees to the people sitting on benches in the pit below them, they were outside the proscenium and got a slanting view of the stage. The people of quality sat in private compartments or 'boxes', just as on Sundays, when they went to church, they shut themselves off from the common herd in box pews. The middle-class playgoer now sat in the pit and the one-time 'groundlings' – the poor people, including the coachmen and footmen who had brought the quality to the theatre and would take them home afterwards – were relegated to a high gallery at the back of the auditorium.

The curtain, unknown in Elizabethan days, had come in with the Restoration, but only in the Kembles' time had it started to be used during the play to denote the end of an act. There was a good deal of painted scenery, and designers were skilful in using perspective to suggest depth and distance. Illusion was helped, too, by holding the performances in the evening by candlelight.

Another difference, of course, was the disappearance of the Elizabethan boy actors. King Charles had insisted that female parts should be played by women, so that when Sarah began her stage career there was already an established tradition of actresses for her to follow – which was sometimes an encouragement but just as often a nuisance, when audiences expected her to play a part exactly as it had been played by some popular predecessor.

In one respect the Kemble Company followed just the same practice as Alleyn's and Burbage's; they wore the everyday costume of their own period. Cleopatra appeared in a hoop skirt and Antony departed to war in the scarlet tail coat, white breeches, and cocked hat of a Hanoverian general. This did not mean that the dressing of a play was rendered cheap or simple, for everything had to look good of its kind and a dress must not be seen in a different play the following night, so an extensive wardrobe was essential.

It nearly always *was* a different play the following night. It might be an entirely new one. Actors were expected to be quick students and amazingly versatile, to play comedy or tragedy and to master a fresh part overnight. There might be only two or three rehearsals, there was not much 'type-casting', and nothing so restful as a 'run' of the same play.

It was a hard life, as Sarah's parents had often warned her, and as she had seen with her own eyes ever since she could remember.

Only one thing makes the achievement of the eighteenth-century actor credible to the modern reader – the greater simplicity of the production. There *was* no 'producer' in our sense of a man who directs, corrects, and harmonizes every detail. The plays were largely written in long speeches, often in verse, so that they (and the cues) were easy to learn. The stage was not cluttered with much furniture, so that there were not many intricate moves and groupings to get right. Actors were not continually sitting down, getting up again, or coping with stage properties such as telephones and decanters.

In a sense the attitude of the actor was rather like that of the opera singer as it survived into the twentieth century, when a prima donna, provided she knew her words and the music, was expected to be able to play her role with a company, and in a theatre, she had never seen before. So, in the eighteenth-century playhouse, there was less thought of production subtleties and teamwork. A performance was, at its best, a collection of splendid solo efforts, not an artistic unity except by chance.

Only thus could the plays have gone on, night after night, in town after town. But these limitations did not mean that there was no scope for genius or that the audience was uncritical.

The eighteenth-century audience was intensely critical. It could – and did – howl like a mob, as though the unfortunate players were standing not on a stage but on a scaffold. It threw things; it was prepared sometimes to break up the theatre. And this could happen without the performance's being notably bad, for disturbances could be arranged by the bribery of jealous rivals.

This was the world Sarah chose, and with her eyes open.

To tour under her father's management was probably not the happiest arrangement, especially after all the trouble that had gone before, so in the spring the young couple joined another company, Sarah as leading lady and William as some sort of assistant stage manager, then as now regarded as about the lowest form of theatrical life. It was a third-rate company, anyhow, exploited by its two shark-like promoters, Chamberlain and Crump.

Summer found them playing at Cheltenham, a spa still

in its infancy and not yet to be named in the same breath as fashionable Bath. It had, however, a few visitors of quality, among them Lord Bruce and his intellectual step-daughter, the Hon. Henrietta Boyle. Seeing from the play-bills that there was to be a performance of Otway's famous old tragedy, *Venice Preserved*, his lordship thought it would be amusing to take along a party, if only to laugh at the ranting and posturing of these unknowns. The ladies and gentlemen got a surprise.

Poor Sarah was tired and out of sorts. She had already realized that she was the main breadwinner – it would always be she who would have to keep William, rather than the other way about – and her first baby was to be born in the autumn. When she heard that an elegant party of titled folk were taking their seats in a box, and that they sounded as if they had come to giggle rather than to enjoy the tragedy, it was the last straw. She went on the stage in a mood of black despair.

But already – as all her life – Sarah was a professional. Each new audience was a challenge. One never surrendered. She threw herself into her part with all her usual passion and fire. Strange, disturbing noises came from Lord Bruce's box. She assumed that the ladies and gentlemen were in fits of barely suppressed laughter, but she disdained to give one glance in their direction. Somehow she got through the evening.

It was not until the next morning that she learnt of her mistake. The explosions had not been of mirth but of genuine emotion – for eighteenth-century audiences were far more open in the display of their feelings when they were deeply moved. It was not unknown for women to faint or for men to weep. The idea that it was unmanly to do so came in only with the nineteenth-century conception of the 'stiff upper lip'.

Sarah's performance had staggered Lord Bruce's party. It was not just her remarkable beauty, it was the intensity and conviction, the passion with which she played her part. When she cried despairingly:

> *'Whither shall I fly?*
> *Where hide me and my miseries together?'*

the listening ladies had felt an anguish no less than that she was portraying. By the end of the fifth act, when the distracted Belvidera died after seeing the bloodstained ghosts of her husband and his friend, the Hon. Henrietta and her companions were themselves ready to expire, and their gentlemen escorts were in hardly better case. Afterwards the ladies had scarcely slept all night and their eyes were still red with the violent sobbing which Sarah had so mistakenly imagined to be stifled laughter.

This news was like balm to Sarah's wounded feelings, but something better was to follow. Miss Boyle came to visit her and express her admiration. More than that, she turned out her own wardrobe and gave Sarah dresses, shawls, and other accessories invaluable to a penniless young actress. It was the beginning of a lifelong friendship between the two.

Lord Bruce, too, was keen to help in his own way. He

wrote off to David Garrick at Drury Lane – the foremost actor-manager in England. Sarah's hopes soared. If she could get to London, her fortune was made. The days passed. It was learnt that Garrick had been interested enough to send down an experienced actor, who had watched her performance without disclosing his identity and had then returned to London with an enthusiastic report on her talent. But more days passed, and weeks, and the post boy did not bring the eagerly awaited letter from Garrick. The company moved on. At Wolverhampton Sarah gave birth to a boy, whom they christened Henry. Soon she was hard at work again, acting for another company at Liverpool, and still there was no word from Garrick. Lord Bruce's kindness had accomplished nothing.

Disappointed, she did not despair. She wanted to succeed, yes. Fame was part of success. But cheap publicity never appealed to her. The thing that mattered, apart from having enough bread to eat, was to act to the very limit of her powers.

It was in that year that she made her great discovery. She learnt how to 'get inside a part' in a newer and deeper sense than she had believed possible – how to act with her brain, as well as with her voice and hands and those expressive eyes.

In later years she dated it all from a particular evening, an experience she never forgot. She was to play Lady Macbeth the following night. She waited until everyone else had gone to bed and then settled down to learn her lines, which she knew would be easy, because it was not a long part compared with those she often played. The whole incident gives a very good idea of the way in which the actors of the period approached a new role. They felt that there was little to it beyond learning the words and then reciting them with all the usual tricks of tone and gesture.

That night, for all her efficient memory, Sarah found it impossible to memorize the lines. Instead, she fell completely under the spell of the character. Lady Macbeth became terrifyingly real. Lady Macbeth possessed her. At last, excited to the brink of panic, Sarah rushed upstairs and, without stopping to undress, flung herself on the bed beside her sleeping husband. Even next day she found it strangely difficult to make herself word-perfect. But somehow she got through that first performance of *Macbeth* and knew that she had learnt something even more important than the lines.

Garrick had not forgotten the promising unknown, but, with three experienced and popular leading ladies already in his company, making endless trouble with their jealous rivalries, he had to bide his time before he could introduce a newcomer. He kept track of Sarah, however, and in August, when she was once more in Worcester, he sent down another 'talent scout' to see her as Rosalind in *As You Like It*. This time the scout was a clergyman, the Rev. Henry Bate. The choice was less curious than it sounds. Mr Bate, like many other eighteenth-century parsons, had various interests besides his religion. He owned a newspaper, *The Morning Post*, and was greatly attracted to the theatre. He was a pugnacious boxer, and, as if fists were not enough, was prepared to fight duels like any other gentleman of his time.

Rosalind was not one of Sarah's best roles. She never really shone in comedy and she disliked a part which required displaying her legs in male disguise. None the less, her performance pleased Mr Bate, and at long last came the offer from Drury Lane. There was a rival offer from the other London theatre, Covent Garden, for whispers of this new girl had brought other scouts to watch her, but William (who handled all Sarah's business arrangements) accepted Garrick's. It was modest enough, three pounds a week for Sarah, two pounds for himself.

Now there was a further delay before they could go to London, for Sarah was expecting another baby. They continued with their tour, Sarah acting as long as possible, and at Gloucester, on 5 November, a daughter was born, whom they christened Sarah Martha. Less than two months later, on December 29, 1775, Sarah made her London début as Portia in *The Merchant of Venice*.

Again, it was not an ideal role for her. Portia was too cool and controlled, had too much sly humour, to suit an actress who excelled in passionate tragedy. Sarah's newness to the London stage, her youth and beauty, did not save her from the unkindness of the critics. Only one newspaper had a good word for her performance, and that, not surprisingly, was *The Morning Post*.

Garrick, though, was patient. He was getting to the end of his own career. For thirty-five years he had dominated the English theatre. Whatever might be said by his enemies (and he had plenty) – that he was con-

ceited and quarrelsome and a snob – no one could seri-
ously deny that he was a great actor, a master of his craft.

Sarah's modesty and seriousness, her anxiety to learn,
must have appealed to him as a refreshing relief from the
incessant squabblings of his other actresses. No doubt,
too, he took a malicious pleasure in building her up as a
possible rival to them in the days to come. He coached
her himself and, on the evenings when she was not playing, reserved a box for her so that she could sit and study
his technique. Sarah seized the chance gratefully. She had
no desire to waste her free evenings on frivolous social
activities – all her life she preferred quiet genuine friendships with a few people to the crowds and compliments
of the fashionable set, and in any case, at this point in
her career, she was not famous enough to be sought after.

So, for two years she worked patiently at Drury Lane,
learning all the time from Garrick's tuition and example,
but still making little impression on the public. Then
came the announcement she had dreaded: Garrick was
retiring at the end of the season, handing over the
management to the playwright, Mr Sheridan, and two
other men, who would reopen the theatre after an
interval during which the players would make their own
arrangements to 'rest' or tour the provinces.

Garrick assured William that there was no cause to
worry. His wife's talents – and of course his own –
would not be overlooked by the new management. That
was true enough. Unluckily, those talents did not greatly
attract the partners. William was written off as useless,
only worth employing if it was unavoidable. And Sarah's

gifts were not displayed to advantage in the artificial kind of comedy which most appealed to Sheridan. What scope for her tragic passion was there in *The School for Scandal*, to be presented for the first time in the new season at Drury Lane?

The Siddonses had no sooner reached Birmingham for their first provincial date, at the theatre in New Street, than a letter overtook them from London. It was regretted that their services would not be required again and that their contracts could not be renewed.

It was a bitter humiliation. Sarah felt that she had been a failure in London, that she had been, as she said, 'banished from Drury Lane as a worthless candidate for fame and fortune.' Things were not, however, as bad as they looked. She was still young, but she had matured as an actress, thanks to those two years with Garrick. And though she might feel in her heart that she had failed, that was not how she appeared to others. To the audiences in Birmingham and Liverpool, York and Manchester, she brought the glamour of the capital. She had played with the great Garrick. No one could ever take away the label, *'late of Drury Lane'*.

After a year or so in the northern cities she was offered a permanent contract at Bath. Bath, with its elegant and cultivated public, was the next best thing to London. It had the first Theatre Royal in the provinces. There was another in Bristol, only twelve miles away, under the same management, and there was an ingenious though exhausting system under which the company were whisked to and fro in fast coaches to play in the two cities on alternate days. The Bristol Theatre Royal, the oldest surviving in England, preserves for us the type of playhouse Sarah knew, though in one respect it was different from the others: it was the first to be built with a semi-circular auditorium instead of a square or rectangular one.

It took time to win over the fastidious theatre-goers of these western cities. Sarah had to play small parts and comedy parts. Only on Thursday evenings in Bath was she given her chance to shine in tragedy – and that was the normally 'dead' evening when the theatre was half empty and everyone who mattered was at the weekly ball. She rose as usual to the challenge. The word went round that Bath now had an outstandingly powerful actress. Soon the theatre was full and it was the dancers who began to look sparse on the floor.

It was a strenuous time-table. Monday morning, rehearsal in Bath, then drive to Bristol and play there. Tuesday back to Bath. Wednesday Bristol . . . and so on through the week, with continual packing and re-packing, mislaid costumes, and new parts to learn. These she usually studied between midnight and three o'clock in the morning. And after the birth of Maria in 1779 there were three small children to be cared for. Another, Frances, was born in the following year but did not live long. Babies often did not, even in the best-regulated families at that period. To have an actress mother can hardly have improved their chances. But Sarah could not stop working. The livelihood of them all depended on her.

Among the visitors to Bath during those years was Mr Sheridan's father. He told his son how Sarah had conquered all hearts there and soon the famous playwright was trying to lure her back to Drury Lane. She did not yield at once, but the mere invitation took away much of the past bitterness. At last she said yes. On June 19, 1782, she gave her farewell performance to the sorrowing playgoers of Bath, a mere seventeen days after the birth of another little daughter, Elizabeth Ann. Then it was farewell to Bristol too, and a long seaside holiday with William and the children at Weymouth. At the end of the summer they went up to London and took lodgings convenient for the theatre at 149 The Strand.

So much, so very much, depended upon this second attempt to conquer London. There was no hope of a third chance.

Four years of popularity in the West Country had given her self-confidence, but it wilted now that she approached the scene of her former failure.

Everyone fussed round her with well-meant advice. Her father came up to London to be with her in the time of trial. William plodded round the coffee houses and taverns of Fleet Street, trying to arrange favourable publicity in the newspapers, and possibly doing more harm than good. When Sarah wished to make her first appearance in a play called *The Grecian Daughter*, old Mr Sheridan persuaded her to choose rather *Isabella, or The Fatal Marriage*, in which he had seen her act in Bath. This advice was good. The part of Isabella was full of pathos. Her audiences in Bath had always wept copiously. If she could not move Drury Lane with this, she never would in any play.

There were three rehearsals. At the second, as she gained power, she had the rest of the cast in tears and the realism of her death-bed agonies was altogether too much for her son Henry, who was now eight and old enough to play the part of Isabella's child. Back in her lodgings, she found to her horror that she was losing her voice. She went to bed utterly exhausted and slept through until noon the next day, missing the last rehearsal. Wisely, they let her. She knew her part. It was rest she needed, for voice and nerves alike.

One more day of waiting . . . Then the performance. Mr Kemble came to call for her and take her to the theatre. William was nowhere to be seen. The most charitable explanation was that he might perhaps be buying drinks for the critics.

When the curtain fell amid riotous applause – and an excited theatre audience in 1782 was hard to distinguish from a real riot – elderly playgoers vowed there had not been such an evening since Garrick had made his first appearance as Richard the Third, forty-one years before.

Again Sarah went to bed speechless and limp with exhaustion. When she woke, there were the newspapers to convince her that her triumph had not been a dream.

'This accomplished woman,' she read, *'beyond all comparison is the first tragic actress now on the English stage.'*

True, that was in her old friend, *The Morning Post*, but the other papers, which had been prepared to be hostile, were just as warm in her praise.

She was twenty-seven and the London theatre was at her feet.

During the half-century which followed, Sarah became by degrees a living legend. She conquered society. The King and Queen saw her in all her parts, summoned her to the palace, and honoured her with the nominal appointment of 'Preceptress in English Reading' to the princesses. The Prince of Wales (later Prince Regent and King George the Fourth) stood godfather to her son, George John, who was born in 1785. She was invited to stay at Windsor.

Most of the great men of the time came under the spell of her acting. She went to tea with old Doctor Johnson and they talked of the English drama. The young poet Byron thought there was no one like her. The chief artists of the day buzzed round her like bees – Gainsborough, Reynolds, Romney, Lawrence, and many more. At one period she was sitting for her portrait to no less than three of them. The playwrights buzzed round her even more annoyingly, pestering her to accept their master-pieces. One was Bertie Greatheed, who brought her a dull tragedy in verse. Reluctantly, but remembering his mother's past kindnesses at Guy's Cliff, Sarah appeared in it, but not even her genius could save the piece from oblivion.

For nearly twenty years she played at Drury Lane. Her

great Shakespearean roles were Queen Katherine in *Henry the Eighth*, Constance in *King John*, Desdemona in *Othello*, and – the supreme achievement of her whole career – Lady Macbeth. Much of the time she was in non-Shakespearean plays, many of them deservedly forgotten. By no means all her parts suited her – she was unwise to play Rosalind again, and Ophelia, though tragic, was far from ideal for her – but no criticism could shake her position now.

Drury Lane became, for a time, quite a family affair. John Philip Kemble gave up any notion of becoming a priest and joined his sister, proving himself an actor and manager of immense ability, with an influence on the theatre no less than hers. Sarah did her best to launch her sisters too. They were snatched away from their dress-making and millinery and brought up to Drury Lane, but they had no great talent and soon disappeared into obscurity again. Only John Philip was in Sarah's class. When in 1802 he took over the management of the rival theatre, Covent Garden, Sarah moved with him and spent the last ten years of her active career there.

No one could be so successful without making enemies. The very brilliance of her death scenes brought anonymous letters alleging that she had attended the death-beds of strangers merely to study their last agonies and reproduce them on the stage. On the other hand, when she failed to reach the death-bed of one of her daughters in time, she was accused of callousness. The truth was that she had been in Ireland and that the girl's illness had been kept from her, and when at last word reached her, a week of violent storms prevented all sailings across the Irish Sea. Her shyness was taken for coldness and pride. She was never one to enjoy the gossip and mischief-making of the backstage world, and her reward was to be made a target for it by those who envied her.

Worst of all, she was libelled and cartooned as being mean over money. 'Lady Sarah Save-all' was the nickname her enemies tried to stick on her. It was true that Sarah saved. Her ambition was to save £10,000 so that she could retire. The money was collected, but it was a long time before she stopped working. She remained the breadwinner. William, increasingly rheumaticky, irritable, and useless, did little but handle the money and make her a moderate allowance. There were six children to provide for – Henry to be educated at Charterhouse and sent to study in Paris before being launched on the stage, Sally and Maria to be boarded at school in Calais, and the younger ones brought on in their turn. And there was a household to run, at first in Gower Street and then in Great Marlborough Street; and her old parents to help when they came and settled near Sadler's Wells. And there was the future, when her strength failed and she could act no more.

Sarah was neither grasping nor miserly, but she was hardly to be blamed if she was economical with her earnings.

Between London seasons she loved to escape into the peace of the countryside, staying with friends or renting a cottage in the Thames Valley near Oxford. She toured too. She could not afford always to be on holiday when the London theatres were closed, and she could not refuse her adoring public in the provinces. On one visit to Ireland she was able to meet an old friend from the early Cheltenham days, Henrietta Boyle, now Mrs O'Neill and mistress of a magnificent castle overlooking the waters of Lough Neagh. Sarah went back to Bath and Bristol also – but the circumstances of one Bristol visit were unhappy. It was the climax of a great family trouble, in 1798.

Her two elder daughters had come home from school in Calais five years before when the French Revolution led to war between the two countries. Both were striking girls. They brought with them an exciting aura of adventure and a fascinating foretaste of the new fashions and hair styles introduced by the Revolution. Being also daughters of the famous Mrs Siddons, they had a considerable impact on London society.

Thomas Lawrence, born twenty-four years earlier in Bristol, had just become principal portrait painter to the King and the most fashionable artist of the day. Sarah had known him since his boyhood. He was a frequent visitor to her house and was painting her picture for the Royal Academy's summer exhibition of 1797. He fell in love with Sally, by then twenty-one, and a very sweet, gentle character, who soon came to feel about him in the same way. This did not suit the younger and more temperamental Maria, now eighteen, who set out deliberately to steal Lawrence from her sister – and for a long time, thanks to her great attractions and a complete lack of scruple, succeeded.

The end was tragic for everyone. Maria was soon stricken down by tuberculosis, made worse by rushing out on cold winter evenings to secret meetings with her lover, and then still further aggravated by the unventilated sickroom which doctors in that age prescribed. After some months she was moved down to Bristol, to be nursed in the house of one of Sarah's old friends. When the theatres closed for the summer of 1798, Sarah took the rest of the family down there and rented a place near by.

The young painter had by this time seen through Maria's scheme. He had gone back to his first love, and Sally had forgiven him. But Maria, even in the shadow of death, was selfish to the end. She used moral blackmail to extract a promise from her sister that she would never marry Lawrence – and forced her to repeat the promise solemnly before witnesses, including the exhausted Sarah, who had been nursing her devotedly for the past two weeks and in that time had only twice properly undressed to go to bed. Sally could do nothing but obey. Maria died a few hours afterwards, and, though Lawrence went almost mad with fury, Sally kept her word. Five years later she too died, and it was her death-bed which Sarah could not reach in time.

So there was abundant sorrow in her private life. She had lost four of her seven children. Henry, the eldest, was to die too in early middle age, but not before he had married and provided her with three grandchildren. Young George had a family of seven, and as he was out in India, where it was unhealthy for white children, she saw a good deal of these and found consolation in watching them grow up. She had Cecilia, too, the 'baby' of her own family, who stayed single as long as Sarah lived.

Sarah had begun her career before the British public had heard of George Washington. She was queen of the stage throughout the days of the French Revolution and the wars that followed. Her official farewell came in 1812, the same year as Napoleon's retreat from Moscow, when his star too began to set.

The choice of role was obvious for that final appearance. It must be Lady Macbeth, the part she had virtually created, the part which no actress could ever study again without remembering 'the incomparable Siddons'. It was a brilliant occasion at Covent Garden, every ticket sold long beforehand, all London society streaming into the theatre, jewelled and plumed, out of the midsummer sunset glow. When she made her last exit, after the sleep-walking scene, the whole house rose in emotional clamour. This must be the end of the performance. Tonight, nobody was interested in the further doings of Macbeth and Macduff. The management bowed to the will of the public. After twenty minutes of tumultuous demonstration the curtain rose once more so that Sarah, now changed into white satin, could make her personal farewell.

Thousands of people signed petitions that she should return to the stage and she did in fact make several later appearances on special occasions, the last of all being in a benefit performance for her young brother Charles in

1819. She was then within sight of her sixty-fourth birthday, a much greater age in those days than it is now.

She lived exactly twelve years after that last appearance, a stately, grandmotherly figure, deferred to not only by her grandchildren but by all who were privileged to enjoy her formidable friendship. Much of her retirement was spent in a charming country cottage with lattice windows and honeysuckle, not far from where Paddington Station stands today. In those days Westbourne Green was really green. It was in Paddington churchyard that she was buried in June 1831, and though the family had intended 'a quiet funeral', discouraging the fashionable crowd who would otherwise have turned up in force, a multitude five thousand strong came to see the burial of one who had for fifty years been a legend in her own lifetime.

4. Verdi, Maestro of the Opera

It was 1814, the year before Napoleon's defeat at Waterloo but the year in which the French Emperor's dominion was really collapsing about his ears. Italy, like most of Europe, was in chaos, as the armies of Napoleon's enemies came flooding in to 'liberate' his former subjects – and, in the process, to rob and murder all who were unlucky enough to get in their way.

One day, in the poor little hamlet of Le Roncole, in the dusty plain of northern Italy not far from the River Po, a bloodthirsty troop of cavalry spread terror among those peasants who had not escaped into the fields and hidden themselves in time. Carlo Verdi's humble wine-shop and grocery store was ransacked. Even the people who had sought refuge in the church were pursued there by the drunken troopers. When the foreign soldiers rode off, they left Le Roncole a village of mourning.

Signora Verdi had fled with the other women, clutching her baby son in her arms. Fortunately she had not joined the crowd in the church. Instead she had climbed the bell tower, which, like many Italian bell towers, stood quite separate from the main building. High in the belfry, remote from the horrors being enacted below, she had crouched with her baby. Her lucky choice of a hiding place probably saved for the world one of its greatest operatic composers.

Giuseppe Verdi had been born on October 10, of the previous year, and registered not as 'Giuseppe' but as 'Joseph', the French form, because it was in the period of the French administration. Now that was over. Italy, which for a few years Napoleon had welded into one country, was split again into half a dozen fragments and handed back to its old masters – the hated Austrians, the King of Naples, the Pope, and the various grand dukes, who were really Austrian puppets. Le Roncole lay in one of the smaller states, the Duchy of Parma. Giuseppe grew up a subject of the Duchess Marie-Louise, who had been given the territory because, although she was Napoleon's wife, she was an Austrian princess by birth and had to be provided for when he was exiled to St Helena. Giuseppe, of course, like his parents and everyone else in Le Roncole, was pure Italian, but there was then no nation, 'Italy', to which they could belong.

This is a vital fact to remember. An age of patriotic struggle lay just round the corner and it was to have its influence on Verdi's music.

Meanwhile, that interest in music showed itself very early. As a child Verdi had to serve the parish priest at the altar. Suddenly the organ began to play. It was the first time he had ever been conscious of it and the sonorous music held him spellbound. 'The water,' whispered the priest. Then again, more impatiently, 'The water!' Verdi made no move. He heard nothing but the organ; his duties were completely forgotten. *'The water!'* whispered the priest for the third time in desperation, and gave the boy a push which sent him tumbling down the altar steps with such a crash that he fainted. Almost his first remark on regaining consciousness was to ask his anxious father if he could study music.

That was not easy in a little place like Le Roncole and in a family who were as poor as the peasants around them. But the boy's obsession with music was certainly remarkable, whether it was the music of the primitive old church organ or that produced by a wandering fiddler outside the tavern. The father did what he could. When Giuseppe was eight, he gave him a battered spinet which he had picked up cheaply and which a kind neighbour repaired for nothing. He arranged for lessons from the village organist. So that Giuseppe should get some regular schooling, and not grow up like many of the other children, unable to read and write, he sent him to lodge with a shoemaker in the town of Busseto, three miles away.

Busseto was a pleasant little town, lying between Cremona, famous for its violins, and Parma, no less famous for its violets. Busseto had a battlemented castle, a cathedral (for in Italy there are many cathedrals), and a town square where the band played on Sundays. Verdi must often have missed hearing the band because, when he was only twelve, he took over his old teacher's post as organist at Le Roncole. This meant that on Sundays and feast days he had to walk home and play for the services there. Once, in the early hours of Christmas morning, he stumbled into one of the deep irrigation channels which criss-cross the North Italian plain, and he would have been drowned if a peasant woman had not rushed to help him out. For trudging all these miles in all weathers he received a fee which (with weddings and funerals included) brought him a grand total of about four pounds per annum.

'I had a hard life as a boy,' he said in later years.

His father had been right to send him to Busseto. Small though the town was, it was a wide world compared with Le Roncole, and, being Italian, it had many music lovers among its few thousand inhabitants. Besides the band there was the Philharmonic Society, its conductor being Provesi, the cathedral organist, and its president Antonio Barezzi, the local grocer, who played the flute, the clarinet, and the old-fashioned wood-wind instrument called, from its shape, a 'serpent'. Barezzi was a friend of Carlo Verdi's and took an interest in his boy. Signora Barezzi, alarmed by a murder in the district, suggested that young Giuseppe should come to lodge with them. Giuseppe was happy enough to move. The Barezzis had a pretty daughter, the daughter had a piano . . . very soon Margherita and Giuseppe were playing duets and some of the pieces were of his own composition.

The boy now became an apprentice in Barezzi's grocery business, but his master saw that his real bent was for music. He talked the matter over with the cathedral organist. Provesi agreed. Young Verdi ought to have his chance to study in a great city like Milan, with its Conservatorio and famous opera house, La Scala. But where was the money to come from? The Verdis had none to spare for such an adventure. Barezzi and Provesi put their heads together. A grant was obtained from a local charity. The kindly grocer made up the rest. In the early summer of 1832, a tall pale youth of eighteen, with serious grey eyes and the first sproutings of a dark brown beard, took the road for Milan, some fifty miles or more away.

Milan was the provincial capital from which an Austrian viceroy, taking orders from the Emperor in Vienna, governed the broad territory of the Lombard plain. The black-and-yellow flag flew on public buildings, the hated white-coat soldiers talked German as they swaggered along the spacious streets, but, for all that, Milan remained a city of proud, resentful Italians, continually conspiring against their foreign rulers and ever ripe for revolution. Even a boy whose head was full of music could not fail to notice the strained, sultry atmosphere of the place.

At first, though, a disappointment of his own drove out all other thoughts. The Conservatorio refused to accept him as a student. He was long past the maximum age for admission, which was fourteen. His previous musical training was sketchy, they did not think much of his piano-playing, and his rough country manners made a poor impression at the interview. The examiners were not unfair, nor were they blind to his good points. His musical theory was weak, but if he worked hard at it he might do very well. They advised him to take private lessons with Lavigna, an excellent musician who held an appointment at the opera house.

So, for two years, Verdi studied hard under Lavigna, mastering harmony and counterpoint, getting to know the works of Bach and Beethoven, Haydn and Mozart, and not neglecting the earlier composers of his own country, like Palestrina. Short of money though he was, he must often have visited the opera and listened to the music of contemporary composers then dominating the stage – Rossini, Bellini and Donizetti. Lavigna was kind to him, inviting him to his home when he was not himself engaged at the theatre, and no doubt Lavigna's position there brought the young man an occasional free ticket.

La Scala was, of course, only one of many places in the city where he could widen his experience of music. There was the smaller Teatro Filodrammatico, there was the immense cathedral with its wedding-cake architecture, there were other churches with choirs and organists, there were concerts, there were military bands, playing with a precision seldom heard on the dusty little square at Busseto. Verdi never despised brass bands. His early familiarity with this form of music had a lasting influence upon his compositions.

Gradually the lonely student began to be noticed. He was asked to help out by taking a rehearsal of Haydn's oratorio, *The Creation*, for the Philharmonic Society, whose conductor had not arrived. They were so pleased with the result that he was invited to conduct the actual concert, and then two repeat performances, one at the palace of the Austrian viceroy. After this success, the Society's president commissioned him to write a cantata for an approaching wedding and the Teatro Filodrammatico asked him to set the libretto for a new opera, *Oberto, Conte di San Bonifacio*. But before he could get far with this or develop the other new contacts he was making in Milan, he got word from Barezzi, urging him to return to Busseto.

Old Provesi had died. The post of cathedral organist was vacant. Who was better qualified to fill it than Giuseppe Verdi? It was a splendid opening. With Barezzi's influence behind him, the young man could hardly fail to get it. After all, the organist's salary was partly paid by a contribution from the town council, and in musical matters Barezzi and his friends *were* the town council.

Things did not work out so simply. The church authorities were not going to be dictated to – and there was another organist applying for the post, with the recommendation of two bishops. They gave the job to the other candidate, and at once (as had happened over and over again in Italian history) the little town was rent with a bitter feud between cathedral and council. The latter stopped their financial contribution and paid it to Verdi, for whom they invented a new and high-sounding office as 'Master of Music to the Municipality of Busseto'. Insults flew backwards and forwards, partisans resorted to physical violence and legal action. Verdi's sympathizers gave up going to the cathedral services. The Franciscan friars (who by tradition tended to side with the people against bishops) allowed Verdi's early religious compositions to be played in their church when they were banned in the cathedral, and the Franciscan church was crowded as a result. This whole controversy, which for a little while made Busseto as stormy as the Verona of Romeo and Juliet, had a lifelong effect on Verdi's religious views. He never lost his faith but he always maintained a rebellious attitude towards the authorities of the Church.

Meanwhile, though he had failed to get the cathedral post, he had a livelihood of sorts. His friendship with Margherita Barezzi had deepened into love, her father gave them his blessing, and on May 4, 1836, they were married. A daughter, Virginia, was born in 1838 and a son, Icilio, in the following year. For the moment fate smiled upon them all.

But not for long. The little girl died. Then, the three-year contract with the town council being finished, the young Verdis moved to Milan, taking the opera score which he had at last completed for the Teatro Filodrammatico. Alas, during his long absence, the man who had commissioned it had resigned from his direction of the theatre – and Verdi's good friend and teacher, Lavigna, had died. Even when La Scala took over the opera, the young composer's troubles were not over. The tenor fell ill and the production was postponed.

The outlook was black indeed. Verdi was ill. Sometimes he could not find the rent for their shabby quarters near the Ticino Gate. Once there was not time even to write and borrow it from his father-in-law, for the mail went to Busseto only twice a week. Margherita went out and sold the few bits of jewellery she possessed. It seemed hopeless to stay in the city. Verdi was on the brink of surrender and return to Busseto when a messenger knocked on the door. The great impresario, Bartolomeo Merelli, wished to see him at the opera house at once.

'I have heard your music well spoken of,' said Merelli, when Verdi presented himself. 'I am willing to produce *Oberto* next season.' And he proceeded to outline terms which, though they might not seem generous to us, were very fair by the standards of 1839.

Merelli had heard about the opera from some of the cast in the postponed production. One of these was a gifted young singer, Giuseppina Strepponi, herself the daughter of a composer and a product of the Milan Conservatorio, where (since she was just two years younger than Verdi) they would have been fellow-students had he ever been accepted there. Peppina (as she was called for short) was a generous-hearted woman. She was already working to pay for the schooling of her younger brothers, their father being now dead, but she could also exert herself for a musician who was still no more than an acquaintance. Owing to the postponement she did not herself take part in the production of *Oberto*, but that it ever went on was due largely to her persuasion of Merelli.

Oberto was no masterpiece, but its few performances brought Verdi a certain reputation, the beginning of a long association with the music publisher, Ricordi, and a contract with Merelli for three more operas. Unfortunately, Merelli decided that Verdi's next effort should be a comic opera – a plan to which the young composer agreed most reluctantly. He was in no mood for comedy during the tragic months of 1839 and 1840. In the former year he lost his little boy; in the latter his young wife followed their two children to the grave. At twenty-seven Verdi saw his whole life in ruins around him. The complete failure of the comic opera, a few months later, was the last straw.

'I gave up hope of finding consolation in my art,' he recalled afterwards, 'and I made up my mind to abandon composition.'

For a little while Verdi returned to Busseto, to Margherita's parents, but there was no comfort there, in a place so full of sad reminders, and no livelihood unless he became a grocer. He had not given up music, only composing. He could make some sort of living in Milan as a teacher, so back he went to the city.

Merelli had not lost faith in him. He behaved with tact and sympathy. As Verdi insisted, he agreed to cancel the contract for the future operas which now, the young man vowed, would never be written. Merelli had other views, but he did not voice them. Nobody could drag Verdi from the black depths into which he had sunk. He would emerge in his own good time, and then a helping hand must be ready, but it would need to be offered delicately.

So, for a time, a lonely young man walked the streets

of Milan, his face thinner and paler than ever, his aquiline nose even sharper, his grey eyes mournful. Back in his cheerless room he passed the hours reading trashy novels—he who from boyhood had founded his literary taste on Shakespeare and the Bible.

Then, one snowy evening, he ran into Merelli, who was hurrying to the opera house. 'Walk along with me,' said the impresario, seizing his arm. All the way to La Scala, the cunning Merelli poured out his own troubles. He was in difficulties over a new opera. He had a magnificent libretto by Verdi's friend Solera, a young poet who had previously helped him by touching up the script of *Oberto*. The theme was a grand one – Nebuchadnezzar and the captivity of the Jews in Babylon. Yet for some unaccountable reason the composer Nicolai did not like the libretto and would not start work on it.

They reached the theatre and the warmth of Merelli's office. The impresario brandished the poet's manuscript. 'Here it is!' he exclaimed. 'Solera's libretto. Such a beautiful subject! Take it – take it along with you. Just read it through.'

'What am *I* supposed to do with it?' said Verdi. 'I don't feel like reading librettos.'

'It won't kill you. Just read it, and let me have it back.'

Out of politeness Verdi took the manuscript home. The last thing he wanted to do was read it. He threw it crossly down on his writing table. It fell open and a single line caught his eye:

'*Va, pensiero, sull' ali dorate.*' ('Go, thought, on wings of gold.')

He was struck by the beauty of the Italian words. He read on. He saw that the poet had based his libretto closely upon the Bible. He was tempted and turned a page or two. Then, reminding himself firmly of his resolution never to write music again, he closed the manuscript and went to bed.

It was no good. His imagination had taken fire. He could not sleep. He got up, lit the lamp, and read the libretto through from start to finish. Then he turned back to the beginning. Before he finally laid it aside he felt that he almost knew it by heart.

Yet – a resolution was a resolution. In the afternoon he walked into Merelli's office and handed back the manuscript. The impresario eyed him shrewdly.

'Well, isn't it beautiful?'

'Very beautiful!'

'Then set it to music!'

Merelli knew that the moment had come at last – it was safe, it was necessary, to go over to the attack. He came round his desk, rolling up the manuscript, and stuffed it into Verdi's overcoat pocket. Then he bundled the young man, still protesting, out of the office, and locked the door in his face.

That was how Verdi was induced to change his mind and to write *Nabucco*, as the opera came to be called. For the full name was as difficult to pronounce in Italian ('Nabucodonosor') as in English.

Once launched upon his task, Verdi became more and more enthusiastic. Vitality flowed back. Dissatisfied with a love duet in Act Three, he asked Solera to rewrite it.

The poet did not want to be bothered. Imitating Merelli's tactics, Verdi turned the key in the door and refused to let Solera out of his study until he had revised the weak passage in the text. Once the outline of the opera was shaped in his mind, Verdi did the actual writing in three months. Like many musicians, he drew on reserves of past creation. Thus he worked into *Nabucco* a funeral march which he had originally composed for the town band at Busseto.

Merelli was a little taken aback when he learnt that the opera was finished. He had not dared to hope for it so soon. He had gone ahead with his other plans and no less than three new operas were already announced for the carnival season of 1842. He did not see how he could keep a general promise he had made long ago to Verdi, to put on any opera he wrote at two months' notice. *Nabucco* must wait.

Verdi refused to be put off. After his previous numbed apathy he was raging like a torrent newly released. He could not wait to see his work upon the stage, to hear Peppina Strepponi's clear, sweet mezzo-soprano in the role of the villainess Abigail – the first of the great mezzo-soprano parts which were to become such a feature of his operas. He wrote Merelli a violent letter which was unforgivably rude, but Merelli, more than ever certain that he was dealing with a man of genius, refused to take offence. If Verdi insisted, *Nabucco* should be added to the carnival programme. But there was no money left for new costumes and scenery. They would have to manage with what they had in stock.

Rehearsals started late in February. The first performance was on March 9. Verdi watched from a seat in the
orchestra, beside the first cello, according to the practice
of those days. At the end of Act One there was such a
roar from the auditorium that for a few alarming
moments he mistook it for the sound with which
Milanese audiences showed their opinion of bad work.
But he was not long left in doubt. The thunderous
shouting was due to delight. And the performance continued in the same glow of enthusiasm. The chorus of
the captive Jews, that passage which had first kindled the
spark of his inspiration, 'Go, thought, on wings of gold,'
was wildly encored. When the final curtain came down,
both the cast and the orchestra joined with the audience
in giving the composer a tremendous ovation.

Merelli meant to make hay while the sun shone. A new
opera was commissioned, Solera again providing the
libretto. The full title meant 'The Lombards on the First
Crusade', but the work is known simply as *I Lombardi*.
Merelli handsomely left a blank space on the contract for
Verdi to insert his own fee. Verdi, a conscientious and
methodical man in business, was nonplussed. Peppina
Strepponi came to his rescue. She suggested a high, but
not unreasonable, figure. Verdi took her advice and, as a
result, received as large a sum as had ever been paid for
an opera in Italy up to that time.

Before *I Lombardi* could be produced, however, there
was trouble with the censorship. Though the First
Crusade had happened a long time ago, it was a

reminder that once the northern Italians had been a proud, free, fighting people. The chief of police, himself an Italian, wondered whether his Austrian masters would welcome such a reminder. He summoned Merelli, Solera and Verdi to his office. Verdi refused to go. The opera, he said, should be presented as written or not at all. Merelli used all his tact to win over the police chief, who reduced his demands to a single unimportant change. The opera was duly presented and was a popular success.

Verdi's music was in tune with the mood of Italy in the eighteen-forties. It was the time of the great patriotic movement known as the Risorgimento – the 'resurrection' of the Italian people, so many centuries sunk in slavery to foreigners. However remote the subject of a play or novel, the public would twist a topical meaning out of it. When, in Verdi's next opera, *Ernani*, based on Victor Hugo's text, the chorus sang:

'To Charles the Fifth be glory and honour!'

the public soon changed the name to 'Pius the Ninth' and used it as a cue for patriotic demonstrations. Pius the Ninth had just been elected Pope, and everyone was hoping that he would use his new office to unite the separate regions of Italy. A few years later, when similar hopes were centred (with more success) on Victor Emmanuel, the King of Sardinia who became ruler of the whole mainland too, Verdi's name was often chalked on walls as a revolutionary slogan. Everybody knew that

'VIVA VERDI' had also a code meaning, 'Verdi' spelling out the initial letters of *'Vittorio Emanuele Re D'*
Italia' ('Victor Emmanuel, King of Italy'), which at the
time he was not.

Ernani won Verdi the beginnings of a reputation
abroad. His operas were presented not only in Milan and
Venice, Florence and Rome and Naples, but in London,
Paris, and even Vienna, where the Austrian theatre-
goers enjoyed his music without being aware of any anti-
Austrian sentiment underlying it. Verdi by no means
confined himself to themes from Italian history. In 1845
he wrote an opera about Joan of Arc. Two years later his
love of Shakespeare found expression in his *Macbeth*, a
work which broke new ground and startled some people.
For one thing, it contained no love interest. For another,
it called for real acting, not just the straightforward singing which usually satisfied the Italian audiences.

In that same year, 1847, Verdi went to London to
conduct his new opera, *I Masnadieri*. The English
capital made a mixed impression upon him. His first day
there was a typically Victorian Sabbath and 'there was
not a soul to be seen', a depressing introduction for one
who had known only the animated Sundays of the
Catholic Continent. Though it was June, he smelt smoke
everywhere. It was 'like living on a steamboat' – that is,
the smutty little steamboats of the eighteen-forties. The
climate took away all pleasure in work. As he got to
know London better, he liked the city more. He was impressed with its magnificence and wealth – wealth which
he knew that he could tap with his operas, if only he

could bear to live there. 'But I could never stand the climate,' he concluded sorrowfully. 'If only London had the weather of Naples, it would be Paradise.'

He went now to Paris. Here he renewed his friendship with Peppina Strepponi, who had retired from the stage owing to voice strain (she was only thirty-three) and had set up as a singing teacher in the French capital. Her house in the Rue de la Victoire became his second home during the next year or two, when much of his time was spent in Paris, and he used to give her address for his business correspondence. Peppina was charming, intelligent, and practical. Like so many operatic singers of the day, she was by no means a saint, yet contrived to be devoutly religious. Why she and Verdi waited years before marrying is a question which has never been answered. They were made for each other. Now began nearly fifty years of loving companionship, which gradually softened the tragic memory of Verdi's first brief marriage.

He was now entering the fruitful period in which he wrote the first of the operas chiefly associated with his name. In 1851 it was *Rigoletto,* with its now familiar aria, *'La donna è mobile',* ('Woman is fickle'). 1853 saw *Il Trovatore* ('The Troubadour') and *La Traviata* ('The Erring One'), the first being an immediate success in Rome and the second a failure in Venice, though it quickly recovered and established itself with the public.

There were several reasons why *La Traviata* did not immediately please. The heroine was a character with an immoral past, and, though she paid for her sins in the end by dying of consumption, she was represented on the stage by an absurdly buxom prima donna. Further, though we today see the opera as a romantic costume-piece, it was originally a contemporary one, set in the eighteen-fifties. Opera-goers were not used to watching their singers in what was, to them, 'modern dress' – they had come to assume that all operatic stories were taken from some picturesque bygone age – and in this, as in so many other things, Verdi had to fight against prejudice.

These years were full of stress, not only inside the theatre, though even there life seemed a constant battle with an assortment of adversaries, from the censors downwards. There were greater troubles still, outside his professional work. His mother died – and his grief found artistic expression in the mother-son relationship in *Il Trovatore*. While he was completing this opera his father also nearly died. Then, too, there was an unhappy rift with Antonio Barezzi, his former benefactor and father-in-law, who did not look sympathetically upon his association with Peppina Strepponi. Indeed, many of Verdi's old friends in Busseto had cooled towards him.

This was particularly sad because Verdi had bought himself a farm on their very doorstep and was making himself a permanent home in the countryside he had known as a child. It was a medium-sized farm called Sant' Agata, with vineyards and some acres of plough-land. Buying it satisfied some deep instinct in Verdi, the instinct of the peasant stock from which he sprang. And it was no idle hobby, the amusement of a world-famous composer who left all the daily grind to a foreman. He farmed that land himself, with strict attention to every detail. Despite the work of composition, the inevitable correspondence with various opera houses, and the occasional journeys to supervise productions, Verdi's farming stood comparison with that of any of his neighbours.

He was always up at dawn, and before he took his first cup of coffee he would be out for a look at his crops or the horses he took such pride in breeding. It is said that no other musician has ever known so much about horses as Verdi did. Dogs, too, he loved, especially big ones. There was even a tame cock which accompanied him on his drives, to the amusement of the neighbourhood.

Not that the neighbourhood saw much of him. He planted trees round the house and lived like a recluse. He never went into Busseto if he could help it, though he did attend the weekly cattle market in Cremona. Chance callers were not encouraged, but a few close friends were always welcome, particularly the conductor Mariani, who shared his passion for shooting. In March they might go squelching through the snow and slush in the woods along the river, in quest of wild duck. In September it would be quail and partridge. At other times Verdi just walked, rode, drove, or amused himself with a rowing boat on his small artificial lake. Meals and bedtime were early, with cards or billiards in the evening. Peppina had given up her career as a music teacher in Paris. They were married in 1859 at a little village in Piedmont, between Turin and Geneva.

This came at a moment of great importance in the

history of Italy. War broke out between the Piedmontese
– the only independent section of the Italian people –
and the Austrian Empire. After a breathless sequence of
events, packed into about eighteen months, not only were
the Austrian provinces and their satellite duchies (like
Verdi's native Parma) freed from their old governments
and united in a new Italian state, but so was the southern
Kingdom of Naples. For a few years longer Rome and
Venice remained in foreign control, but the rest of Italy
was united very much as we know it today.

These stirring events made their effects felt even on the
quiet farm at Sant' Agata. Verdi was a patriot and a
staunch supporter of the Piedmontese Prime Minister,
Cavour, whose shrewd policies had brought about the
unification of Italy. Cavour now had the difficult task of
forming a new Parliament for the whole country, to knit
together regions which had never been under the same
government since the time of the ancient Romans. He
wanted to get hold of men whose names were familiar to
other Italians, outside their own locality, and what name
was better known than Verdi's? So, on Cavour's insist-
ence, Verdi reluctantly agreed to stand for Parliament.
He was a deputy for five years, attending the sessions in
Turin, the Piedmontese capital which served, to begin
with, as the capital of the new Italy. Politics, however,
were not in Verdi's line, and he was glad to give up his
seat when he felt that he had done his duty.

Meantime his artistic career continued, though sometimes several years passed between the composition of one
opera and another. He was commissioned to write one for

the Imperial Theatre at St Petersburg, then the Russian capital, and twice he made the long journey, with the faithful Peppina at his side, to the far northern city which is now Leningrad. On the second trip he made a short stay in Moscow to see a production of *Il Trovatore*. He liked the Russians, whose polite manners he found genuine by contrast with the insincerity of the Parisians. The new opera itself, *La Forza del Destino*, was not popular – it was too full of gloom and horror and many Russians must have felt that they knew quite enough about 'the force of Destiny' without having it served up to them in Italian opera, from which they expected life and colour. However, the Tsar and his courtiers were warm in their compliments, and Verdi was honoured with the Imperial Order of St Stanislas, as well as receiving a fee of twenty thousand roubles instead of the standard five hundred.

A few years later came an invitation to visit another unfamiliar country. The ruler of Egypt, the Khedive, wished to celebrate the opening of the Suez Canal with the production of a new opera. Verdi refused the invitation. Eventually he was persuaded to compose an opera, *Aïda*, for presentation in January 1871, though he still refused to travel to Cairo himself.

Aïda was more truly Verdi's own creation than any opera which had gone before. No libretto existed, only a four-page synopsis drafted by a French archaeologist friendly with the Khedive. Verdi had to find his own Italian librettist to prepare a full text, and he started work on the music long before all the words were written. It was a collaboration throughout, with Verdi very much the dominant partner, continually making his own suggestions for word and action, either by correspondence or in discussions at Sant' Agata.

The setting was ancient Egypt, the theme designed to please the modern nation just reborn in that country. Aïda, the heroine, however, was an Ethiopian captive slave girl in the household of the Egyptian princess, Amneris. That Aïda was herself the daughter of the Ethiopian king was a fact she judged it wise to keep to herself. Both Amneris and Aïda were in love with the handsome young Egyptian general, Radames, who was chosen to lead Pharaoh's armies against the Ethiopians. Radames was victorious and entered Memphis in triumph, leading a train of captives among whom Aïda recognized her own father, in her emotion almost betraying his identity to the Egyptians. The plot was full of those agonizing situations so dear to grand opera – the jealousy of mistress and slave girl in love with the same man, the conflict of Aïda's heart torn between Ethiopian father and Egyptian lover, and the terrible dilemma of Radames when offered Pharaoh's daughter as bride, the kind of offer which it was suicidal to refuse. So the story went on, with one high-powered scene leading to another, a moonlight tryst on the banks of the Nile, a plan to escape, a treason trial by priests in the subterranean hall of judgment, and Aïda's final act of love and self-sacrifice when she allowed herself to be buried alive with her doomed lover. It was a story which gave full scope for pageantry and monumental scenery, for banners and trumpets and martial glory, dancing girls and chanting priests. And from the famous opening soliloquy by Radames (*'Celeste Aïda'*) to the farewell duet of the entombed lovers, it gave Verdi scope for the most dramatic music he had so far written.

The première was delayed for nearly a year by the Prussian siege of Paris, where the scenery and costumes were being made, and it was not until Christmas Eve, 1871, that the curtain went up on *Aïda* before a Cairo audience which included the ladies of the harem and in Oriental splendour matched the company on the stage. To these Egyptians *Aïda* seemed a splendid evocation of their ancient greatness, but in writing such stirring marches and swelling melodies Verdi is more likely to have been inspired by recent events in his own country. For the Franco–Prussian War, which had delayed the costumes, had also compelled the withdrawal of the French garrison in Rome, and now at last the King of Italy was free to enter that city and make it his capital, to the joy of all patriots.

Aïda was another landmark in Verdi's development. It was a further move towards 'musical drama' as distinct from the purer type of opera, with less real acting, which was traditional. Verdi was accused of imitating Wagner, his opposite number in Germany, who was aggressively proclaiming that this new musical drama was the only worth-while form. Verdi, however, was imitating nobody. He was following, as always, his own natural line with complete independence and integrity. He grew heartily sick of the way in which *Aïda* was discussed and misunderstood, until he could scarcely bear to hear it mentioned.

Was it to be his last opera? As the years passed, it seemed so. He composed a Requiem and other religious music; he revised an old opera, *Simone Boccanegra;* but he accepted no fresh commissions to write for the stage. He did not need money: he was wealthy now and had everything for his own needs and the charities he loved to support. He did not crave publicity or even honour: when the King made him a senator he took the oath but never took his seat, and when a new theatre at Padua was named after him he declined to attend the opening. More and more he buried himself at Sant' Agata with Peppina, his horses, his dogs, and the quiet pastimes of the countryside.

His seventieth birthday came and went. He said publicly that he would write no more operas. 'Music,' he said, 'demands youthfulness of feeling, impetuosity of the blood, fullness of life.' He had no wish to go on churning out work, as other old men had done, long after the public had tired of them.

Yet his mind was still as active as ever, his musical invention as rich, and in his retirement he was meditating a new opera. The brilliant librettist, Boito, offered him a script based on *Othello*. Shakespeare had always fascinated Verdi. Gradually he yielded to temptation, and, as he moved thoughtfully around his farm, the characters of Othello and Desdemona and Iago became almost more real to him than the people he encountered in his daily life. He achieved such an intimate companionship with them that, as he confessed later, it was a sacrifice to share it with the public.

Otello was produced at La Scala in February, 1887, and was a staggering success. Verdi, at seventy-three, had done it again – done it again, that is, not in the sense of equalling earlier work but in his capacity for breaking new ground. *Aïda* had been different, *Otello* was different again. Its use of recitative, its deployment of the orchestra, its inspired interweaving of music and language, showed that the old man was still developing his genius in fresh directions. If the whole world of music saluted *Otello,* the audiences at La Scala felt a special delight. Verdi was theirs. In their theatre he had first budded, almost half a century before. Where else could this last splendid flower have been allowed to bloom?

Incredibly enough, it was not the last flower. Boito set to work on an operatic treatment of *The Merry Wives of Windsor.* Slowly, very slowly, Verdi began to compose the music. It would be called, after the central character, *Falstaff.* It would be a comic opera. It was fifty years since he had written a comic opera, and then it had been a humiliating fiasco. He began his task in 1890 and finished it in 1892. He was in his eightieth year when, in February 1893, the curtain went up at La Scala on this last opera of all.

Being a comic opera, *Falstaff* could scarcely help being 'different' again from what had gone before – but in fact its difference went far beyond the fun and gusto with which it brimmed. They were there in plenty; Verdi had repeatedly said that he was only writing the opera 'for fun', and that light-hearted humour had gone into the score. But there was musical innovation too, with all kinds of technical subtleties to delight the knowledgeable listener. In a sense Verdi, the popular idol, had produced a musicians' opera with many hidden riches which escaped the cheering crowd. But in other respects *Falstaff* had enough general appeal to satisfy them.

Verdi and his wife were getting very old now. They spent the summers at the farm and the winters in a flat at Genoa. In the autumn of 1897 Peppina fell ill. She insisted that it was no more than a bad cold. When Verdi brought her some flowers she complained that she could not smell them. A few hours later she was dead.

The long, loving companionship was ended. Verdi lived on like some old tree, gaunt, solitary, unable to die. He, who had been born when Napoleon was master of Europe, survived into the twentieth century. He spent Christmas, 1900, with old friends in Milan, and there on January 27, 1901, just five days after the death of Queen Victoria, he too died. His funeral was scarcely less of a state occasion than hers, for the composer had long been venerated in Italy as a national hero and two hundred thousand people lined the streets of Milan as his coffin was carried to its resting place. Fittingly, it was the chapel of the Musicians' Home which he himself had established, and Peppina's remains were reburied beside his own.

5. Jenny Lind, the Swedish Nightingale

Silver birches, birds singing, wild flowers that seemed to rush magically into life as the snow melted in the sudden Scandinavian spring . . .

These were among Jenny Lind's first memories, together with the lamp-lit wakenings and bedtimes of the brief winter days, the fragrance and crackling of pine logs in the stove, the shouting of the Ferndal boys, the kindly crooning voice of their mother, and the music which throbbed and boomed from the whitewashed church near by when Papa Ferndal was practising.

Her own mother was someone quite different, almost a stranger, altogether sterner and colder than Fru Ferndal. She came when she could, mostly in the summer. She came from the city. She could not come often or stay very long. There was the school. It kept her so busy. It was better for Jenny to stay here in this beautiful village with the Ferndals.

'School' . . . 'city'. . . The words meant nothing to Jenny. She could remember nothing of Stockholm or the shabby third-floor flat where she had been born and had spent the first few months of her life. The world she knew was this village of Ed Sollentuna, peaceful among its birchwoods, fifteen miles to the north.

She went there early in 1821 – she was born on 6 October 1820 – and she stayed with the Ferndals for nearly four years. Then the cosy little world of Sollentuna cracked around her. She was going back to live with Mamma in the city. Not because Mamma particularly wanted her (the little girl sensed that from the start) but because Fru Ferndal was not well and could no longer keep her. In fact – though this Jenny did not understand until afterwards – Fru Ferndal knew that she had not long to live and she died in the following year.

Jenny never forgot those first idyllic years in the village. They did much to mould her character and tastes. She always loved Sollentuna and went back when she could.

Meantime, the city was a poor exchange. Jenny's Stockholm was not the imposing capital spread out on islands, its palaces and churches mirrored in the waters of lake and sea. It was the limited world of a four-year-old – dark steep staircases, a narrow street outside that was often muddy, dingy shops and workshops – a world where there were no wild flowers and not much bird-song and even the snow turned grey.

Worst of all, Jenny's real mother was, to tell the truth, a poor exchange for the warm-hearted woman who had so far brought her up.

Life had been hard for Anne-Marie Fellborg and it was not surprising that it had made her hard in turn. She had divorced her worthless first husband, who had left her with a baby to support, Jenny's half-sister, Amalia. To earn her living she had started a little private school, taking boarders as well as day girls, all in the cramped quarters of the flat. She had gone back to her maiden name of Fellborg and was still known by it, because of the school, long after she met the man who was to be her second husband and the father of Jenny.

Unfortunately, Niclas Jonas Lind was no solution to her problems, only an addition to them. He was an easy-going, light-hearted drifter – Jenny's most typical recollections of her father were of his pleasant singing in the evening, to her mother's accompaniment on the guitar. But he was out a good deal and exactly what he did for a living, if anything, was not clear. Instead of being able to give up her school, Jenny's mother had to work harder than ever. She had now a man to support as well, and a second child.

Jenny's homecoming was just an added burden to an embittered woman whose nerves were already stretched to snapping point. There was no time to give the child any special attention or try to win her confidence. She must go into the school with the others, though far the youngest, and if she could not understand the lessons at least keep quiet. Bewildered, scolded and ignored by turns, Jenny knew only one thing for certain – that she was a nuisance. She had not even the prettiness which would have made her a pet of the older girls. She was, at that age, a pallid, snub-nosed, homely little creature. These next four years, from four to eight, made another and very different contribution to forming her character.

They gave her a quality which – strangely enough – was to be a powerful ingredient in her appeal: the touchingly wistful air of someone over-sensitive and always insecure, ever seeking to give love and to receive it.

Her half-sister was kind enough, her shadowy father was not ill-natured, but it was the affection of a mother that Jenny wanted and never really found. That gap could never be filled. The only person who could even partly fill it was her grandmother. Old Fru Tengmark lived in the Widows' Home and Jenny was allowed to run through the streets to visit her. She turned eagerly to this grandmother, who had time for her and infinite patience, who would tell her stories from the Bible and listen to her own chatter. Fru Tengmark was the ideal refuge for an unhappy child – restful, comforting, and approving.

When Jenny was eight the school was doing so badly that her mother had to close it and give up the flat as well. She herself got a post as governess in a distant part of Sweden. She could take Amalia with her but not Jenny. What was to be done with *her*? Grandmother could not have her in the Widows' Home, her father was useless in such an emergency. There seemed nothing to be done but answer a newspaper advertisement from a childless couple who wanted a child to look after.

This time Jenny's luck was in. By a happy coincidence the advertiser proved to be the caretaker at the very institution where Grandmother lived. The caretaker and his wife had a flat on the ground floor, looking out upon the gay and busy street leading to St Jakob's Church. They readily agreed to take Jenny and for the next year she was happier than she had been for a long time, racing up and down stairs to visit her grandmother and other old ladies who took a fancy to her, and playing with the cat.

She used to sing to the cat. She was so much happier, she used to sing to everybody, including herself. But it was to the blue-ribboned cat she was singing, curled up in the window and watching the passers-by, when she first caught the attention of a maid servant on the pavement. The maid told her mistress – and her mistress was Mademoiselle Lundberg, a dancer at the Royal Opera House close by. Mademoiselle Lundberg sent a message. She would like to hear the little girl sing, if she could be brought to her apartments.

The message caused some consternation. Jenny's singing might do very well for a cat – the cat had never complained – but singing to Mademoiselle Lundberg was quite a different matter. Also, though Mademoiselle Lundberg was a grand person with a maid and so forth, she was also an actress. The good ladies of the Widows' Home had their own decided views about the wicked lives led by people on the stage, and there was no doubt that the opera house of that period produced more than its fair share of Stockholm scandals.

Neither Grandmother nor the caretaker's wife had to make the awkward decision because just at that moment Jenny's mother paid one of her regular visits. And she, though as strait-laced as the older women, was also hard-headed. She had a scheme to restart her school in fresh premises. A contact with someone at the Royal Opera

House might bring her pupils. It would be better not to snub this Mademoiselle Lundberg. So she dressed up Jenny for the occasion and took her along. When Jenny had performed, the dancer said:

'The child is a genius. You must have her trained for the stage.'

She was not joking. She was emphatic. The schoolmistress was staggered. It would not have been tactful to voice all the objections at the back of her mind. It seemed sufficient to indicate the practical difficulties. Mademoiselle Lundberg retorted that there need be no practical difficulties. She would give them an introduction to the Director. If the authorities agreed with her estimate of Jenny's talent, they would take care of the financial side.

Driven into a corner, the mother came out with her further objections. She could not let her daughter be exposed to the moral dangers of the theatre. Mademoiselle Lundberg begged her to go away and think it over carefully. She did so – but Grandmother only strengthened her fears. Fru Tengmark, for all her gentleness, had the rigid standards of her generation. The theatre was the home of falsehood and pretence, and its performers (she firmly believed) carried all their fictitious wickedness into their private lives off-stage. She could not bear the thought that her sweet innocent little Jenny should be launched upon this slippery slope to perdition.

Mademoiselle Lundberg did not give up the struggle. She got Jenny's mother to agree, reluctantly, to a voice test by the singing master, Herr Craelius. Surely there was no harm in that? It committed them to nothing. Again Jenny was arrayed in her best. On the very threshold of the Opera House, an imposing eighteenth-century building on an open square close to the water-front, her mother's prudery nearly forced her to turn back. But they went on, up the broad steps and into the magnificent foyer. Soon they were being greeted by a kindly old man with curly hair and craggy features whom, from the first, even Jenny found quite unalarming.

She sang an aria from *The Sacrificial Feast* by the German composer, Peter Winter. When she finished, Herr Craelius's eyes were moist. He must, he said, consult the Director: he himself had no authority. He went off and told the Director he had discovered a child of remarkable promise. 'How old?' demanded the Director, who was a member of the nobility and a very grand personage in Stockholm. 'Nine, my lord.' '*Nine!* The Royal Theatre is not a kindergarten!' Herr Craelius was well aware that the usual age for admission was fourteen at least, but he himself was in sight of retirement and he was determined not to miss the chance of training Jenny. He told the Director that, if he would not admit the child, he himself would take her as a private pupil without charge. Impressed, and no doubt nervous of missing a future star, the Director agreed to hear her sing. He too was deeply moved by the quality of her voice. He offered a long-term contract of the usual type. In return for training and maintenance, on terms which overcame the mother's lingering scruples, the Opera House would have an option on Jenny's services for a considerable time afterwards. It was a gamble whereby the Opera House staked its money on likely pupils and, when they turned out well, got first-class young performers for moderate salaries.

It was all down in black and white, even to Jenny's pocket money of about a shilling a week. A full stage training – not only singing but dancing and acting – would be provided by Herr Craelius and his staff in the studios on the second floor of the Opera House. But it was not an ordinary school with general subjects, and still less was it a boarding school. Pupils were boarded out and their ordinary education paid for. As Jenny's mother was moving back into Stockholm and starting a school again, Jenny would now return to her – but she would be paid for housing and teaching her own daughter. The Opera House even supplied a piano for Jenny's practising. To complete her mother's satisfaction with the arrangement, she was asked if she would take three other girls on the same basis. At one stroke of the pen, Fru Fellborg was assured of the minimum income needed to establish herself in the city once more.

Jenny began her training as a 'student actress' a week or two before her tenth birthday. She loved it. She at once showed talent as a dancer. Within a few months she had made her first stage appearance, dancing in a melo-drama about a robber chief. A newspaper wrote glow-ingly of her *'verve and self-confidence'*, her *'complete lack of shyness'*. She worked with amazing keenness and concentration. Old Craelius knew just how to draw the best out of her. He retired after a year but never lost interest in her progress as long as he lived. His successor, Herr Berg, was just as enthusiastic. If anything, he worked her too hard. From occasional small parts in the Opera House she was promoted to singing duets with him at concerts. By the time she was thirteen she was making more than twenty public appearances every year.

Work Jenny did not mind. Life at home was not so happy. She and her mother had never achieved a warm and understanding relationship. She would have been better boarding with anyone else and learning her general lessons from any other teacher. To make matters worse, she had the embarrassment of witnessing, every day, the friction between her mother and her senior fellow-students, who found Fru Fellborg anything but a congenial landlady.

In the end it came to open mutiny. The three older girls marched out and carried their tale of woe to the matron at the Opera House. She heard them sympathetically and let them move into some vacant rooms on the top floor of the building. Before very long, just three weeks after her fourteenth birthday, Jenny had a violent scene with her mother and stormed out to join her friends. The matron allowed her to stay, and for nearly two years, until the summer of 1836, Jenny defied parental authority from her stronghold in the attics of the Royal Opera. The whole incident has an extremely modern flavour and shows that at least some young girls were acting with remarkable independence even in the year before Queen Victoria came to the throne of England.

Jenny's mother wanted Jenny's money, whether or not she wanted Jenny. She had the law on her side and she did not hesitate to take the case to court. The rebel had to give in and go home. But Jenny had the comfort of knowing that it was not for ever. Final freedom was in sight.

She was nearly sixteen, a slender girl of about five feet four, fair-haired, with only her big grey eyes and mobility of features to redeem her from downright plainness. But when she opened her mouth and sang she produced a voice of exquisite purity, with a heart-rending pathos which matched her wistful appearance.

That year she was allowed to make her début in grand opera in a work by a living Swedish composer who soon became one of her personal friends. In the following January she was promoted to the grade of 'actress', and her student's allowance was increased to the modest 'salary' of sixty pounds a year, with an additional fee for each performance. Little more than a year later, on 7 March 1838, she was given her big chance. She was allowed to sing the leading role in Weber's romantic German opera, *Der Freischütz*, of the innocent young heroine tragically shot by her sweetheart with one of the magic bullets the Devil has taught him to manufacture.

Dramatically and musically, the part was ideal. Jenny could identify herself with it heart and soul. It was her limitation, all her life, that she could not portray characters morally repugnant to her. Weber's music gave full scope for the special excellences of her singing voice, that range and purity and effortless birdlike quality which

Jenny Lind

Henry Irving

won her, from the beginning of her career, comparison with a nightingale.

The audience had known her for seven years, as child and student and small-part player. They were friendly but not prepared to be impressed. Jenny overcame all the disadvantages of familiarity. The thunderous ovation at the end would have satisfied a visiting prima donna. 'Local girl' had indeed 'made good'.

It was characteristic of Jenny's religious disposition that she went down on her knees in her dressing room. She had discovered the wonderful power within her and she never doubted that it was a gift from God which it was her responsibility to use properly. She felt that her whole life was changed. She said later: 'That morning I woke up one person, and at night I went to bed another.' She used to celebrate the anniversary as her 'second birthday'.

That autumn her real birthday, her eighteenth, brought her independence. The law allowed her to leave home and live with friends, which a year later she did. Though her mother, and on occasions her father, sometimes accompanied her on trips to sing in other towns, she could not stay under their roof without frequent arguments and scenes. Herr Lind was amiable enough but feckless. The main trouble was with her mother, who had no glimmering of Jenny's real nature and saw her musical triumphs purely as a means of money-making. Jenny was a gold mine to be worked for the benefit of the family – her parents, that is, for poor Amalia, the only one who might have appreciated her, had died several years earlier.

Between 1838 and 1841 Jenny dazzled the musical public of Sweden in opera house and concert hall alike. In Meyerbeer's *Robert the Devil*, Donizetti's *Lucia di Lammermoor* (with its famous mad scene), and Bellini's *Norma*, she took over one by one the roles in which she was to be most popular throughout her career. In *Norma*, especially, she attracted the notice of the critics by an interpretation of the character quite different from that of singers who had played the part before.

Norma is the high priestess of a Druid temple in ancient Gaul in the age of Caesar's conquest. For some time she has been passionately but secretly in love with the Roman proconsul, Pollio. Heedless of her vow of chastity, heedless too that Pollio is a leader of the enemy power occupying her country, she has carried on a love affair with him and two children have been born without anyone's suspicions being aroused. Some operas abound in this sort of improbability. The opening scene, in the Druids' sacred grove, tells the audience that the Gauls are plotting a patriotic revolt – and also that Pollio is tired of Norma and has fallen in love with another virgin of the temple, Adalgisa, the contralto. Then Norma, still unaware of the full truth, mounts the altar steps and sings the great soprano aria which is the only part of the opera now familiar to many people, the exquisite invocation to the Moon, '*Casta diva*',

'Chaste goddess, may thy silver beam—'

praying that her lover may be led back to her.

In the next scene Adalgisa confesses to Norma, as her superior, that she has broken her vows. Norma, with her own guilty conscience, is about to grant her absolution when she realizes that Pollio is the man concerned – that Adalgisa is the rival who has taken her place. The drama mounts, with rumblings of armed revolt as a background to the emotional turmoil of the two young women. Norma is willing to give up her lover to Adalgisa, if Adalgisa will adopt the two children. Adalgisa is too loyal to accept Norma's sacrifice and tries vainly to persuade Pollio to return to his first love. Then Norma, who has hitherto tried to hold back the rebels for the sake of her lover, summons the warriors with three furious strokes on a brass shield and – Boadicea-like – proclaims all-out war against the Romans. At this moment Pollio is dragged in, caught in the act of breaking into the temple to abduct Adalgisa. The penalty is death, but as the pyre is built up on which to burn him alive, she tries to save him by confessing her own sin. At the climax of the opera Norma steps into the flames, and Pollio, conscience-stricken at last by his own treachery, throws himself after her.

Earlier singers had played Norma as a more sinister character, terrible in fury at her own betrayal – something more like Medea in Greek tragedy. Jenny was quite incapable of portraying anything so completely foreign to her own nature. She concentrated on the self-sacrifice of Norma, on her concern for her children, on her remorse at her own lapse from virtue. Her interpretation was accepted. Some declared that 'Casta diva' had never been sung in the proper manner before. But whether she was singing these great romantic roles in the theatre – or Pamina in *The Magic Flute*, Donna Anna in *Don Giovanni*, or a host of roles in other operas now forgotten – or Haydn's *Creation* at a charity performance, or Swedish folk songs in some fashionable drawing room, whatever the occasion, she seemed to cast her enchantment upon all.

She worked too hard. Apart from her duties at the Opera House, she could not bear to say 'no' to people who begged her to sing for good causes. It seemed so wonderful to be able, just by singing, to bring money streaming in for orphans and old people and the sick in hospital. Her mother did not share her pleasure. Charity, in her view, began – and stayed – at home. Jenny ought to be making money for herself—that is, for all of them. She should ask for a raise at the Opera House, she should agree to a raise in ticket prices when she performed in Uppsala or Gothenburg. Jenny, however, always hated any increase of that kind.

Her voice began to show signs of wear. She was worried. Sometimes she found it hard to sustain her high notes. Overstrain revealed itself in hoarseness. Her teacher, Herr Berg, could not help her. An Italian colleague advised her to go to Paris. There was a Spanish singing master there, Manuel Garcia. He could give her the advanced training which she now needed and which no one in Stockholm was competent to give.

She could not go to Paris at once. She had to fulfil her obligations at the Opera House, she had to save money for the journey, the fees, the expenses of living in France. She had to wait until the midsummer of 1841, when she was within three months of her twenty-first birthday.

To most girls of that age, especially coming from a small Scandinavian city, Paris would have spelt excitement and gaiety. But Jenny never liked Paris, never liked France at all. She saw it as a frivolous, wicked, immoral place, the exact opposite of all she believed in. She nerved herself to go there because she must consult this man Garcia, but she could not have felt less enthusiasm if she had been entering a lion's den.

No lion could have been crueller than Garcia at their first encounter.

'It would be no use teaching you, mademoiselle,' he said. 'You no longer have a voice.'

He explained that her whole system of breathing was wrong. She had been trained all along on incorrect lines. At each successive performance she had been steadily damaging her voice. And she had been doing it for years.

She listened with horror. It was impossible to deny the truth of what he was saying. He could back his statements with inescapable scientific fact. Garcia had really studied the physiology of the vocal organs. In the world of music in 1841 he was exceptional in his scientific approach to singing.

Jenny did not despair. She was upheld by her simple faith that her voice, besides being admittedly the product of a certain physical structure and process, was also a gift from God and destined to be used. She extracted a grudging promise from the Spaniard: if she would rest for six weeks, not singing a note and talking as little as possible, he would give her a second audition.

The six-week silence was easier to bear in that foreign city than it would have been at home. Jenny was living in a boarding house. She filled her days with visits to museums and art galleries and occasional theatres, though she had to watch her expenditure. She explored the old quarter and the banks of the Seine. She poured out her loneliness in long letters to her friends in Stockholm. Above all, because she never lost her faith that her career would go on, and that as an opera singer she would need foreign languages, she spent hours on French and Italian. Rules, exceptions, word lists . . . she sat in her room throughout those stuffy weeks of July and August when, at its best, Paris can be unbearable, covering dozens of foolscap sheets.

Towards the end of August she went for her second audition. Garcia listened intently, then gave his verdict. He was prepared after all to take her as a pupil – if she, in turn, was prepared to go right back to the beginning. She might have been a prima donna in Sweden, but with him she must go back to singing scales. His fees were twenty francs an hour.

Jenny bowed her head. What did the humiliation matter? Or the high cost of the lessons, which would force her to find cheaper lodgings? She would sing again. Garcia, she felt confident, was the one man who could help her.

Ten months of gruelling work with him transformed her vocal technique. Her breath control was prodigious.

She could hold a note for what seemed, to fascinated audiences, an eternity – but an eternity of delight, because that high-soaring soprano was of such poignant and spiritual loveliness. She had no more to learn from Garcia. He had taught her certain vitally important things. These, combined with her natural endowment, her earlier musical and dramatic training, and her own tireless industry, enabled her to return to Stockholm with her voice not just restored, nor even improved, but transmuted into something of an altogether higher quality.

She went back to the Opera House on the same modest terms as she had left it, a basic salary of about three pounds a week. When she made her reappearance on the stage, in her favourite role of Norma, four days after her twenty-second birthday, the directors soon realized how wise – and how lucky – they had been to re-engage her. The performance was a triumph. The whole season was an extended triumph. Jenny became more than ever the idol of Stockholm, the favourite of society from the Royal Family downwards.

Success could not spoil her. She was shy in company and hated publicity. She was absorbed in her art, her own simple private religion, her work for charities, and her strong personal friendships.

So far there was no question of marriage. Some of her deepest affection was stirred by men already married – first Adolf Lindblad, the Swedish composer, and later Mendelssohn – and for Jenny, with her strict principles, there was no question of letting these feelings get out of hand. Hans Andersen became her devoted friend, but she could never see him as anything more, though the Danish writer, for his part, was romantically in love with her almost from their first acquaintance. Jenny had certainly no prejudice against marriage. Often, amid the weariness and exhaustion of her very successes, she longed for someone to fall in love with, someone who would relieve her of her burdens, but for a long time there was no sign of the right man.

Every Swedish woman, until she married, had to have a legal guardian to help her with her financial affairs. Usually she appointed her father. But Jenny, as she saw her fortunes prospering, had no wish to see them at the mercy of her feckless father, especially as that would really have meant her grasping mother. She therefore asked a friend, Judge H. M. Munthe, to act as her guardian. A kindly man, honest and tactful, an amateur singer and violinist of great talent, Munthe played his part with sympathy and devotion. For many years he acted as a buffer between Jenny and her parents, with their incessant demands for money and their complete failure to understand her interest in charities. She saw to it that they lacked nothing. She gave them an allowance and finally settled them in a house they asked for at Sollentuna, but they were never satisfied. For ten more years, until her mother died, Jenny was continually nagged and reproached as an ungrateful daughter. It was a great sorrow in her life, because she believed fervently in the Fifth Commandment and her conscience pricked her even when her reason told her that she was right in her attitude.

In these years Jenny established herself as a prima

donna famous not only throughout Scandinavia but also in Germany and Austria, then the dominant countries of the musical world. She became friends with the Schumanns, Mendelssohn (who first roused her interest in oratorio), and many other great figures of the day. It is hard for us today to imagine the effect an outstanding performer had upon the music-loving public in the mid-nineteenth century. Sometimes the crowds serenaded her hotel window or unharnessed the horses to draw her carriage through the streets, while when she left a city the students would storm the room she had vacated and make themselves rosettes from the bed linen. Newspapers gave her the space which today is given only to athletes or murderers. Kings and queens – even in the etiquette-ridden courts of Germany – received her with no less warm friendliness than the students, although perhaps more quietly.

Jenny, admittedly, made a particularly strong impact. Though she had no real beauty to reinforce her superb voice, she conquered by sheer magnetism. 'She's a witch and always will be,' declared a woman friend from Stockholm who met her unexpectedly in Germany. 'It's utterly impossible to see and hear her and be in her company without becoming bewitched and enchanted, and falling completely in love with her.'

But if 'Jenny Lind fever', as it was called, raised the temperature of enthusiasm to unique levels, it is only fair to remember that in this period any outstanding performer could win a degree of honour and respect beyond anything known today. Television, radio, records, and films were still unknown. There was only one way to hear a great artist, and that was to get inside the building where he or she was performing – at no matter what cost for tickets or what physical risk when the crowd fought to get into the cheaper seats. There was only one way to see what these rare and wonderful creatures looked like – for there were no photographs in the newspapers, only (sometimes) printed portraits in the shops. To see what Jenny Lind and the other great ones looked like in the flesh, thousands of people were glad to stand waiting for hours in the streets. The arrival of a prima donna in a provincial town electrified the place as only a royal visit could today. Thus, when Jenny came to England and visited Norwich a few years later, she stayed in the bishop's palace and the church bells of the city were rung till midnight by the delighted people.

It was some time before she was able to make her début in England. The manager of Drury Lane, a certain Mr Bunn, had approached her in Berlin when she was tired and overstrained, and had talked her into signing an agreement to appear in London. Jenny signed unwillingly – and foolishly – and immediately afterwards regretted it. She was always shy of new theatres and especially of new countries. She felt she could not cope with England and the unfamiliar English language. She wanted to postpone the visit indefinitely – or for ever. So she did nothing, persuading herself that the agreement was not legally binding, because it had not been approved by her guardian.

Six months later, in the summer of 1845, Queen

Victoria and the Prince Consort visited Bonn for the
ceremonial unveiling of a statue to Beethoven in the town
of his birth. Other royal personages gathered for the occasion. Besides the public concerts, there were some exclusive court functions for the visiting notables. Jenny performed, and at once won the hearts of Victoria and her
husband. Singer and sovereign were young women of the
same age. They shared not only many musical tastes
(Victoria was a Mendelssohn enthusiast) but also a pious
and basically serious attitude to life. When the royal
couple moved on up the Rhine to spend a few days at a
castle near Coblenz, they took Jenny with them as their
guest. And when they said good-bye to her, Victoria added
in her emphatic way: 'I hope I shall see you in England
some day.'

She was not alone in that hope. The next year Jenny
received an offer from Mr Lumley of Her Majesty's
Theatre in London, an opera house in keen competition
with Drury Lane and Covent Garden, both of which were
partly controlled by Mr Bunn. It was a splendid offer.
She was to be paid £4,800 for the season, with the free
use of a furnished house, a carriage and pair. As for any
lingering fears that, if she set foot in England, Mr Bunn
would sue her for breach of contract, Mr Lumley would
take care of Mr Bunn. Jenny was of two minds, dazzled
by the terms, yet still nervous of England in general and
of Mr Bunn in particular. Mendelssohn advised her to
sign and she did so.

This was by no means the end of her fears and hesita-
tions. There were more delays. Letters flew to and fro.

Mr Lumley found he could *not* appease the furious and disappointed rival Mr Bunn. Would Jenny come to England? If she did, what would happen? If Jenny was nervous, poor Mr Lumley must have been on the verge of a nervous breakdown. His season was planned and publicized, one by one his three other prima donnas fell ill, and still there was no Jenny. Then at last, on 17 April 1847, she arrived.

She was to make her first appearance on May 4, in one of her favourite parts, Alice in Meyerbeer's *Robert the Devil*. The intervening two weeks were a long-drawn anxiety for all concerned. Jenny attended a performance at Her Majesty's Theatre. She was alarmed by the size of the building and by the splendour of the fashionable audience, with its flowers and jewels and the scores of elegant gentlemen in full evening dress. Britain was then at the zenith of her wealth and greatness. Her capital city was the unchallenged centre of the world. These people, who riveted their opera glasses upon her in the interval, as soon as she was recognized – these people were expecting so much. Could she give it to them? As happened over and over again in her career, she suffered an agonizing lack of confidence, then braced herself and accepted the challenge.

When the day came, not only she but all London seemed feverish with excitement. The colonnaded theatre near Trafalgar Square was besieged. Single seats had been booked at six pounds each. Society people jostled for the unreserved places in the humble pit. The Queen, her husband, her mother, and the Queen Dowager, Adelaide, appeared in the royal box just before the curtain went up.

As usual, Jenny rose to the tremendous occasion and triumphed. Welcomed almost hysterically at her first entrance, she tamed the audience with the exquisite beauty of her voice, imposing a rapt silence upon them so that they listened spellbound until at last their applause could be unleashed. Then it sometimes went on for twenty minutes at a stretch. When she took her final curtain calls before a wellnigh delirious audience, the Queen snatched up her bouquet and threw it down across the footlights at her feet.

In fact, it was not just a few flowers but England that was soon at Jenny's feet. The Queen and Prince Albert came to the theatre every time she sang. On the Queen's birthday they attended with nine state carriages and a flashing escort of Life Guards, while inside there were trumpeters to greet them with a fanfare and Yeomen of the Guard to stand sentinel at the edge of the stage. Jenny was invited to sing at Buckingham Palace. Victoria gave her a nightingale of jewels to wear in her hair.

Parliament was no less enthusiastic. Three times the House of Commons had to adjourn, because so many M.P.s had gone to the opera that there was no quorum to carry on the debate. When Jenny decided to take up riding, sallying forth from her new home in Kensington to join the fashionable parade in Hyde Park, the gruff old Duke of Wellington was proud to be her escort. Every class of society was enslaved by her charm.

There were, of course, individuals who stood out

against it. One of them was Mr Bunn. He threatened legal action and finally brought it. Jenny lost the case. She had to pay £2,500 damages for breach of contract, as well as heavy expenses.

Long before this unhappy and worrying affair was settled, Jenny had fallen in love with the country which she had come to with so many forebodings. Just as she had found the character of Victoria especially congenial to her, so she found the whole atmosphere of Victorian England in harmony with her own attitude to life. Perhaps she would settle here? Sweden was dear but small, too much of a backwater. France she hated. If she did not make her home in Germany, where better than England?

Settle she must. Her health and nerves would never stand a lifetime of exhausting journeys and operatic performances. The career of a prima donna was not really to her taste. Though one side of her nature seemed to be fulfilled when she held the stage with her artistry, another and perhaps deeper side was continually troubled and frustrated. To her beloved grandmother the theatre had always seemed a den of iniquity. To millions of other respectable people it still seemed so. Though Jenny's own experience had shown her that it need not be, she often wondered uneasily whether it was the right sphere in which to use the gift she regarded as sent to her by God.

The idea of giving up the stage was nothing new. She had spoken of it to friends long before she came to England. Now it gained strength. It was reinforced when she went on tour in the provinces and discussed it with the Bishop of Norwich. More and more she felt that she should quit the make-believe world of the theatre. She could still use her voice on the concert platform and in private houses, especially in oratorio. She could still make a living for herself and her dependent parents. She could still raise money for the charities and scholarship funds which were so dear to her heart.

She could do nothing sudden, however. She had her obligations to the disappointed Mr Lumley. And whether or not she had an obligation to the theatre-going public – who would be stunned by the retirement of their idol before her thirtieth birthday – she knew that it was in opera they wanted to see her and that the change was a gamble. Before she gave up the stage she must work a little longer and collect the considerable sums needed to put her charitable schemes and her own family affairs on a safe financial basis.

So, for a year or two, she combined the old life with the new. She still packed the theatre – she even took on a new role in the opera *I Masnadieri* when Verdi came to London to conduct it. She made a start in oratorio, singing the soprano part in *Elijah* which Mendelssohn (whose recent death had just come as a great shock to her) had long ago written with her in mind. She appeared all over England at concerts, in which she was joined by a young German-Jewish pianist, Otto Goldschmidt, destined to play an ever more important role in her private life.

That private life had just reached a turning point. Jenny had been engaged for some time to an old colleague of the Stockholm opera house, a handsome German-

Swede named Julius Günther, but it was difficult to maintain a relationship between two temperamental artists usually hundreds of miles apart, and the engagement was broken off. Jenny now went to the other extreme. She fell in love with a dull young man named Claudius Harris, a captain in the Indian Army with so little interest in music that he went to sleep when she sang, and with a dreadful mother who abhorred everyone connected with the theatre. Jenny's friends shook their heads. The outlook for such a marriage was black indeed. But Jenny went ahead with the wedding preparations.

The day was fixed for May 16, 1849. On the 10th Jenny made her theatrical farewell in *Robert the Devil*, the opera in which she had first conquered London two years before. When the curtain rolled down for the last time, the applause was as tumultuous as then, but few of the cheering audience could really have grasped the significance of the moment. Jenny's stage career was over. And she was still only twenty-eight.

A week later came the wedding day. But the marriage never took place. At the last moment Jenny saw the madness of it all. Captain Harris too had lost his first enthusiasm. They broke off the engagement by mutual agreement. '*I should soon have gone out of my senses,*' Jenny wrote to a friend, '*and was well on the way to doing so.*'

Jenny crossed to Paris, where her good friend Judge Munthe joined her from Stockholm and helped her through the first few painful weeks of readjustment. She went on into Germany, where a specialist warned her

Anna Pavlova

Anna Pavlova in the Swan costume of her
most famous rôle

that she must rest completely, and not sing for six months, if she was to escape a breakdown.

In November she returned to the concert platform and sang in Hamburg. Her accompanist was Otto Goldschmidt. She was drawn to him because he had been a pupil of her beloved Mendelssohn. They talked together of the dead composer. Otto persuaded her to do something she had been unable to do since his death – to sing his songs. And in leading her back to Mendelssohn's songs Otto also introduced her to a whole new field of German romantic music, with which she now enriched her repertory. Otto had been Jenny's devoted admirer since, as a seventeen-year-old student, he had first heard her sing in Leipzig. But the difference in age and religion made a gulf between them. Could it be bridged by music alone?

Meanwhile a fresh adventure beckoned Jenny. She was invited to tour America. The invitation came from that remarkable showman, Phineas Barnum, who made up for his ignorance of music by his unequalled knowledge of the public. Barnum – later famous for the circus he established and made 'the Greatest Show on Earth' – was virtually the inventor of publicity methods as we understand them today. He was ingenious, unscrupulous, and daring. Nothing was too costly, nothing too impudent. Barnum was a genius in the field of promotion. Once he got the assurance from other people that Jenny was the greatest soprano alive, he could not rest until he had presented her to the American public.

Jenny was in the United States from autumn 1850 until

May 1852. She travelled thousands of miles by railroad and paddle-steamer, singing in innumerable cities and towns, and even visiting Cuba. Barnum handled the arrangements with his usual flair, which alternately amused and shocked her. When she was too exhausted to appear on her hotel balcony, Barnum got rid of the crowds below by taking out another woman dressed in Jenny's bonnet, veil and shawl. Another time, when the press of people round the landing stage prevented her disembarking from the ship at New Orleans, he played the same trick to shift them, disguising his own daughter for the purpose. Faced with the same problem at Cincinnati, and knowing that he could not use the device again, he resorted to a double bluff. He went down the gangway with Jenny herself, while an accomplice shouted: 'It's no go, Barnum! You can't pass your daughter off as Jenny Lind this time!' The waiting multitude roared with laughter. They did not budge from the landing stage for another half-hour, by which time Jenny and Barnum were miles away.

Jenny did not quite realize how much she owed to this extraordinary man. Half-way through her American visit she ended her association with him, and thereafter managed her own affairs. The latter part of her time in the States was by no means so successful.

One thing, however, made up for all her business worries. Otto Goldschmidt came over to replace her previous accompanist, who had to return to London. Otto proved the perfect accompanist, a brilliant musician in himself yet in complete harmony with her own personality. That harmony, it became more and more clear, went beyond their music and pervaded every part of their lives. Difficulties were brushed aside, though only after anxious heart-searching. Though a Jew by birth, Otto was not one in practice, and was prepared to become a Christian. Did it really matter that he was several years younger than Jenny? On February 5, 1852, they were quietly married in Boston by a bishop of the Episcopal Church, and in May they set sail for home.

But where was 'home' to be? For a time they considered Germany. They spent most of the next few years there, touring the concert halls. In 1853 a son was born, whom they christened Walter. A daughter, Jenny, followed in 1857, and another boy, Ernest, in 1861. Meanwhile, in 1858, they had decided to settle in England. They lived first at Roehampton and then at Wimbledon, where they built a big house called Oak Lea. Otto needed to be near London – he had his own career, now mainly as a conductor and as a professor at the Royal Academy of Music, but he made time also to look after Jenny's business affairs. She continued to sing and to raise money for good causes. Their house was a centre of musical society, with a constant stream of distinguished guests, but it was also a family home in which the children grew up happily. Sometimes Jenny took them all over to Sweden for holidays to see the country from which their mother came.

The children grew up. Oak Lea became too large for Jenny and Otto. They moved into South Kensington. But Jenny could not stand the city all the year and longed for escape. When her daughter married a man from Herefordshire, Jenny discovered the beauty of the West Midlands. She made herself a summer refuge out of two converted cottages at Wynd's Point, high on the Malvern Hills.

It was a wonderful spot, eight or nine hundred feet above sea level. Westwards she could look across the Wye Valley to the Black Mountains and beyond, forty miles into the deep heart of Wales. Eastwards the Severn Vale spread a brown-green patchwork to the Cotswold Hills. The house itself was embedded in a tree-clad rocky nook, with a pure spring splashing up in the garden and nightingales among the birds that sang. Outside the gate rose the steep grassy Beacon, crowned with ancient British ramparts. All around were woodlands and shimmering expanses of feathery bracken.

Here, in great peace and happiness, Jenny spent a large part of each year towards the end of her life. Otto had to go to London more often, but it was easy enough to drive down the long hill on the Worcestershire side, catch the train at Malvern, and in three hours or so reach Paddington. They kept on the house in Kensington and Jenny gave singing lessons in the drawing room to the students of the Royal College of Music, so newly founded that as yet it had no buildings of its own. The Prince of Wales, later King Edward the Seventh, himself prevailed upon her to become one of its first professors.

In that same year, 1883, she sang for the last time on a concert platform. It was very different from all her previous grand 'farewell' performances. Probably no one realized that it *was* a farewell. It was at the annual concert of the Railway Servants' Benevolent Fund at Malvern. A porter had spoken to her at the station and asked her to take part. Never able to refuse an appeal for charity, and never a person to stand on her dignity, Jenny smiled and agreed.

Only three or four years remained to her. She had taken to spending the winter at Cannes, on the French Riviera, to avoid the worst of the English weather. There, in the early days of 1887, she became ill. Otto cancelled his engagements and hurried out to her, young Jenny followed, and together they brought her home to Malvern, all three knowing by now that she had not long to live. She saw one last summer at Wynd's Point and heard the birds singing round the house just as they had sung round the cottage at Sollentuna, more than sixty years ago. On 2 November she died. She was buried in Malvern, under a slab of granite from her own beloved Sweden, and later a tablet was erected to her in Westminster Abbey, in Poets' Corner, where no woman had ever been commemorated before.

6. Irving, the Great Actor-Manager

The coast of Cornwall might have been made for poetry – for wild, fantastic rolling verse to match the strange sea-chiselled sculpture of the granite cliffs, the soar and sweep of the gulls, the plangent rhythm of the Atlantic, and the brooding mystery of the boulder-strewn wastes that tilt to the skyline.

This was even more true in the early days of Queen Victoria's reign. Cornwall then was a remote Celtic corner to which the first holiday-makers were just beginning to penetrate. A journey from Bristol to St Ives meant not a few hours in train or car but a voyage by paddle steamer.

There, in those days, a boy's voice might sometimes have been heard declaiming poetry against the background of wind and wave. More than one stranger afterwards remembered hearing it. That voice, matured by manhood, was destined to electrify audiences throughout Britain and North America. A faint crackly echo of it can still be heard on one of those ancient wax cylinders which were the forerunner of the modern record. It was, in its day, one of the most famous voices in the world, but the boy's name, John Henry Brodribb, remained unknown outside his family circle.

'I want to be an actor.'

So he once told two small girls with whom he made friends on the beach at Penzance. From his earliest years the ambition was there, but the prospects of fulfilling it were anything but bright.

Johnnie Brodribb lived near St Ives at Halsetown, a newish village of gaunt grey cottages built for the local tin miners. His home was one of the bigger houses, opposite the inn, for his uncle, Isaac Penberthy, was a figure in the neighbourhood, a manager or 'captain of mines'. He was a bearded giant of a man, humorous and wrathful by turns, with exciting memories of his younger days as an engineer adventuring in Mexico.

Aunt Sarah, like her sister, Johnnie's mother, was a devout Methodist. She loathed alcohol and frowned at the miners streaming in and out of the bar across the road. She would have been horrified if she had known that Johnnie's heart was set upon the stage. She wanted him to become a minister. But, for all her strict principles, Sarah Penberthy was no dour, miserable goody-goody. She had as much warmth and humour as her husband.

These two had children of their own, John and Kitty, close in age to their nephew. All four had given him an equally warm welcome when he came to Halsetown in 1842 to make his home with them.

Johnnie's father, Samuel Brodribb, was the son of a Somerset farmer. He had left the land to become travelling salesman for the village store at Keinton Mandeville. There, in a cottage opposite the shop, Johnnie was born on February 6, 1838, in the opening months of Queen Victoria's reign.

It was a sombre period in English history. On the one side there was feverish industrial expansion, with vast fortunes being made; on the other, for the masses, there was abject poverty. For once the law-loving British talked of revolution. Even as Johnnie Brodribb was taking his first uncertain steps across the cottage floor, the starving workmen of South Wales and Lancashire were drilling secretly in the hills with pikes and muskets. As it turned out, the rising never came. Except for one tragic clash with the soldiers in the streets of Newport, there was little violence – though there were deaths innumerable, indeed millions if we include the victims of the Irish famine. For millions more it was a time of hunger, rags, suffering and fear.

Against such a background the decision of Johnnie's parents is understandable. Mr Brodribb could not make a living as a salesman. He sought work in Bristol. His Cornish wife foresaw the hard struggle ahead and feared the unhealthy conditions of the cities in those days. She was determined that Johnnie should grow up in the pure air of sea and country. So, with sorrowful reluctance, she sent him down to her sister.

Thus Johnnie Brodribb, like Jenny Lind, spent many of his early years away from his parents. In his case, however, the bond of affection remained strong. The highlight of each year was the moment when his mother was sighted coming down the gangway of the steamer at St Ives, to fetch him for his regular trip to see his father in Bristol.

Since his mother shared his aunt's disapproval of the stage, it is unlikely that Johnnie told her of his ambitions, or that he was allowed on these annual holidays to enter the enticing portals of the Bristol Theatre Royal. His father did once take him to see a famous lion-tamer, who left a lasting impression on his mind, but his ideas of acting came from the Cornish strolling players, who used to enact gory melodramas in a tent, and from touring productions of Shakespeare in the new Assembly Room at St Ives. Deeply stirred by such performances, which he slipped in to see in spite of Aunt Sarah, Johnnie began to learn long passages by heart and declaim them on his lonely walks along the cliffs.

His other reading was limited to the few books in the house – ballads, the Bible, *Don Quixote* – and to his lessons at a little dame-school in one of the neighbouring cottages. Though he made the most of his educational opportunities, Johnnie was quite as fond of mischief as any of the village children. Once, inspired no doubt by the mummers who used to go dancing and miming round the countryside, he and his cousins dressed themselves up as devils, with horned masks and tails, and went off to frighten an unpopular old woman who was always threatening people with Hell fire. On another occasion he mounted a donkey and rode it through the passageway of the inn.

This Cornish childhood ended in 1848 when Johnnie

was ten. His uncle died suddenly and his aunt found herself poor. Fortunately his father had secured a post in the City of London, with living accommodation provided. Johnnie was now a healthy, well-grown boy, and there seemed no reason why he should not at last be reunited with his parents. With mingled excitement and regret he left the windy moors and cliffs where he had been so happy and set out for the London, where he was to find fame and fortune almost beyond his dreams.

Anyone who has read Dickens can picture the London Johnnie saw in those first days – a London of portly, top-hatted merchants and lawyers, of timid clerks and impudent office boys, of ragged crossing-sweepers, muffled cabbies, and all the other richly diversified types which crowd his novels. Into this labyrinthine city, with its fog and gaslight, its chop-houses and counting-houses, its tenements and thieves' kitchens, stepped a boy from a village where everyone knew everybody else.

Johnnie now went to the City Commercial School, a small but excellent institution with three masters and some part-time visiting staff to teach only thirty or forty boys. The headmaster, Dr Pinches, was a kindlier fellow than his name might suggest. He had a genial round face, with a halo of whitening hair, a progressive approach to education, and, what was most fortunate for Johnnie, a passion for clear and correct speech. Johnnie was inclined to stammer. A bullying teacher might have done him great harm at this stage. Dr Pinches was patient and sympathetic.

Each term ended with Speech Day, when the boys recited before an audience. For one of his first appearances Johnnie chose a blood-curdling monologue about a murderer's confession. It was the sort of melodrama he had learnt to enjoy in Cornwall. But Dr Pinches, listening to the monologue at rehearsal, pursed his small mouth and decided that it was not quite the thing for Speech Day. Young Brodribb had better scrap it and learn a twenty-five-page oration by an Irish barrister.

Johnnie was happier the following term, when he was given a good part in a verse tragedy. Afterwards the headmaster beckoned him forward and presented him to a gentleman in the audience who wished to congratulate him. The gentleman proved to be Mr William Creswick, then playing the lead in *Hamlet* at the Surrey Theatre. Johnnie's pale freckled face must have reddened with embarrassment. He had never seen Mr Creswick, he had never set foot in a London theatre, his mother did not approve . . .

He was not going to let an awkward situation like that arise again. At the first opportunity he tackled his mother. Couldn't he be taken to the theatre? There couldn't be so much wrong with it if the headmaster invited actors to Speech Day. Mrs Brodribb resisted stubbornly, all her ingrained prejudices aroused. The argument raged on. It ended in compromise. She would consent, reluctantly, to Shakespeare. Shakespeare was respectable, even educational. But not even for Shakespeare could she bring herself to set foot in a playhouse.

The unpleasant duty of escorting Johnnie must fall to his father.

Did Mr Brodribb so far forget his paternal dignity as to wink at Johnnie behind her back? At all events, it was not long before the pair of them were off to see Hamlet played by the even more eminent actor, Mr Samuel Phelps, who in the previous seven years had taken over a derelict theatre in North London and made it the home of all that was best in the drama. The name of the theatre was Sadler's Wells.

That first taste of professional acting at its best made an unforgettable impression on the boy. His parents might talk of 'good openings' in City offices. His own determination to become an actor was reinforced tenfold.

It was never far from his thoughts. But he knew that he must be patient. His twelfth birthday came. He was old enough to leave school and earn a few shillings to help his parents, but not old enough to start out on his chosen career. Cheerfully he accepted the arrangements made for him. He became a junior clerk, first to a firm of lawyers off Cheapside, then to an East India merchant in Newgate Street.

Here he made good friends among the half-dozen other young clerks. Mr Blackwell, the senior clerk, was rather a Tartar, but when he was out of the way Johnnie used to entertain his colleagues with dramatic recitations. The office day was long, from half past nine until seven o'clock in the evening, and a break in the interminable pen-pushing must have been welcome.

Johnnie was glad of any audience, however critical – he took their criticisms in good part and learnt from them. But he could do without an audience if necessary. He was always reciting to himself. What he had done on the desolate cliffs of Cornwall he continued to do in the crowded streets of the City, and passers-by turned to stare at the pale lanky youth with the curly black hair who muttered Shakespeare as he strode along the pavement. He was going to the theatre frequently now. He was recalling and memorizing performances he had seen; he was preparing himself to appreciate the play tomorrow night.

When not at a theatre, he spent the evenings at an elocution class or rambled through the foreign quarter with another boy who was trying to learn Italian and French by conversation with organ grinders, waiters, and political exiles. If Johnnie was less interested in the foreign languages, he found great fascination in studying the varied human types, with their unfamiliar gestures and intonations. It was all part of that experience which was needed to enrich an actor's mind.

The early morning was as full as the late evening. In summer he was up at five o'clock to go swimming in the Thames. When he felt he needed more coaching than the elocution class could give, he took private lessons with William Hoskins, a leading member of the Sadler's Wells company, and since an actor was never free in the evening, these were fitted in at eight o'clock in the morning, an almost unheard-of hour for a member of the profession. Hoskins must have been deeply impressed by his pupil or he would never have agreed to it.

But Hoskins undoubtedly *was* impressed. When, after a time, he himself was planning to go to Australia, he invited Johnnie to go with him. Johnnie thanked him but declined. Apart from what his mother would have said, he knew that Australia would not fit into the course he had laid out for himself. Hoskins then offered, since the boy had made such good progress and in any case the lessons must now come to an end, to introduce him to the mighty Samuel Phelps. Johnnie accepted gratefully.

The actor-manager received him graciously, heard him recite, and gave him the stock advice which has been given in all generations to the unknown aspirant: 'Do not go on the stage. It is an ill-requited profession.'

Johnnie stood his ground. Respectfully he made it quite clear that, with all due deference to Mr Phelps's wisdom and eminence, he would not budge from his determination.

Phelps gave him a long, steady look. 'In that case, sir, you'd better come here, and I'll give you two pounds a week to begin with.'

Even in that giddy moment Johnnie did not lose his head. The offer was flattering, but it did not suit his plans. For all Hoskins's coaching, the elocution class, and the fencing lessons he had taken at a school in Chancery Lane, he knew that he was not ready to appear on a London stage. He was not going to jump in at the deep end and perhaps drown. He meant to serve his apprenticeship in the provinces. So, again most respectfully, he thanked Mr Phelps and declined.

Hoskins showed no vexation at his spurning of the

opportunity. Before sailing to Australia he wrote Johnnie a letter of recommendation to a Mr Davis, manager of the New Royal Lyceum Theatre in Sunderland. When Johnnie felt ready to apply for an engagement, this letter would get him one.

Meanwhile, he realized, the young man had still to overcome his mother's opposition. Hoskins went round to see her and, as his last friendly act, put in a reassuring word on Johnnie's behalf. 'One day,' he told her, 'your son will earn fifty pounds a week.' Mrs Brodribb was not persuaded. Though life had been hard and she knew the value of money, her moral objections remained. Johnnie might have made a hundred pounds a week as a burglar, but it would still have been the wrong career.

Johnnie's own attitude is best conveyed in a letter he wrote soon afterwards to a favourite relative, Mrs Wilkins, with whom he often spent his summer holidays in Wiltshire.

'As regards the profession I have chosen I consider it one of the, if not [the,] most intellectual there are. . . . The names of Shakespeare, Garrick, Kemble, Macready and many many others show that they were and are the companions of the master spirits of the ages, and rank as gentlemen and scholars among Royalty and the aristocracy. A person may be as moral and good in that as in any other walk of life. There is much prejudice against it in our circle of society, and that is wearing off as the world grows wiser.'

By the time he wrote this letter he had used his introduction to Mr Davis and been offered an engagement. He had handed in his notice and received the good wishes of his employer and his fellow-clerks – even the stern Mr Blackwell. He had already assured his mother that he would never sully the name of Brodribb, but would take another for the stage. After some deliberation he had chosen 'Irving', and it was as Romeo, in an amateur production at the Royal Soho Theatre on 11 August 1856, that the eighteen-year-old Johnnie Brodribb was first billed as 'Henry Irving'. His letter to Mrs Wilkins was dated a week later and told her of his impending departure to Sunderland.

'I have a difficult task before me,' he told her. But, he added solemnly, *'I have youth and hope, and relying on a higher power for assistance from temptation and surrounding evils, I hope you and all may never be mistaken in, my dear Mrs Wilkins, sincerely yours, J. H. Brodribb.'*

Young Irving, as we had better call him now, needed all his resolution for the gamble ahead.

He was to have no salary until he had proved his value, but he would have considerable expenses. Like all actors in the resident companies of that period, he was expected to eke out the limited costumes provided from stock with his own varied wardrobe, including wigs and accessories. Not only would there be a different play each night (and like minor actors in every age, he might often have to double two or more different characters) but he might be cast in more than one play on a single evening. Audiences had a voracious appetite for entertainment. Performances often began with a curtain-raiser, which the better-class patrons were content to miss so that they could finish their evening meal without haste. When the more expensive seats filled up, it was possible to proceed with the main piece, probably in five acts. Then it was common to provide an 'after-piece', so that a heavy tragedy might be followed by a 'laughable farce', like the ice rounding off a big meal.

Irving knew the demands that would be made on his wardrobe. Though the play was always different, the audience was much the same. There were loud and cruel comments if a particular garment was recognized too often. He had saved about twenty pounds. Out of this he spent boldly, but he dared not spend it all. There was still the fare to Sunderland, far away on the Durham coast. Then, somehow, he had got to live for a few weeks, until Mr Davis decided that he was worth paying.

To add to the problems of budgeting, the theatre was still in the hands of the builders when he got there, and the opening was postponed for ten days, another ten days in which a still-growing eighteen-year-old had to eat. He could not afford to stay in his hotel, so he moved to cheap lodgings on the outskirts of the town, which meant a long walk along the sandy beach, a pleasant enough reminder (while it was still September) of childhood days in Cornwall. After a few days rehearsals began in various public houses, wherever a room could be hired, and he got to know his colleagues. Finally they were able to get into the theatre and rehearse on the stage.

Irving loved it from the start. He wrote to one of the

clerks in his London office that you were *'surrounded by cheerful and happy faces who always greet you with a smile and merry word.'* It was so different from business life – there was *'no restraint on a laugh or joke, no governor to stop your mouth, no petty subjection to one another, because they are equal'*. Actors, as a body, he declared with the confidence born of two months' experience, were *'intellectual, rollicking, good-natured, independent, very polite, knowing, eccentric . . . with one great fault – jealousy.'* Luckily, no one had cause to be jealous of the latest recruit – though some envied the splendidly plumed white hat which he produced for his début as the Duke of Orleans in Bulwer Lytton's blank-verse drama, *Richelieu*.

'Here's to our enterprise!'

That was the first line in the play – and one of the few lines left to the Duke after the drastic cutting of the script. Irving delivered it, draining an empty goblet, as the curtain rose. It was his first utterance as a professional actor, albeit still unpaid. No words could have been more appropriate.

The next night it was *The Lady of Lyons*, a romantic comedy by the same author. Irving had about six lines as a French officer. He had a bigger chance a few days later when he was told to double Cleomenes and Third Gentleman in *The Winter's Tale*. It is said that this performance fell on a Monday and that he could not bring himself to break the Sabbath by studying his parts the day before. At all events, he dried up completely during a speech vital to the explanation of the plot. In desperation he got himself off the stage by inventing a line of his own and bidding his perplexed colleagues:

'Come to the market place and I will tell you further.'

This ingenuity did not bring the reward it deserved. The audience knew what had happened – and soon, through the columns of the local newspaper, so did the whole town.

Mr Irving, wrote the critic, *'utterly ruined the last scene but one . . . He came on the stage without knowing a single word of his part, and although he had his cue pitched to him by the prompter in a tone loud enough to be heard in most parts of the house, he was unable to follow it, and was compelled to walk off the stage amid a shower of hisses.'*

In spite of this humiliation and the newspaper's advice to quit the stage for ever and go home, Irving did not despair. He was encouraged by Mr Davis and two of the older men in the company, who could see the qualities buried under his youthful inexperience. 'If ever I rise, I shall not forget this,' he told them emotionally. Nor did he. Twenty years later, when he had indeed 'risen', he took those two veterans into his London company.

By Christmas he was on the pay roll, earning twenty-five shillings a week. In the New Year, 1857, he got the chance to move on to the Theatre Royal in Edinburgh. He liked the Scottish capital and it provided him with the ideal training ground – an endless succession of parts, experienced colleagues, eminent guest artists, and audiences which included not only critics as blunt as the

Sunderland shipwrights but also a good sprinkling of cultivated intellectuals.

It was a hard life. He worked from ten in the morning until one, two, even three o'clock the next morning. In two or three years he played five hundred different characters, ranging from Macduff and Captain Absolute to the Spiteful Fairy in *The Sleeping Beauty* and Scruncher, Captain of the Wolves, in *Bo-Peep*. In *Hamlet* alone he played half a dozen of the roles.

His reward was to gain immense technical experience and a familiarity with most of the plays in the current British repertory. That familiarity was essential to an actor. With the daily change of programme, there was little time for study and rehearsal. As in the days of Sarah Siddons, a famous guest artist could still descend upon a provincial theatre and expect the stock company to support him without a single run-through. It was their business to know his chosen play already, much as the members of a symphony orchestra are assumed to have a working knowledge of the concert hall favourites.

Irving's instinct had been sound when he had told Phelps that he must serve his time in the provinces. As it was, even when he returned to London, with three years' experience behind him, to appear at the Princess's Theatre, he made no impression upon the public. Soon he was saying good-bye to parents and friends once more, to take up a sudden offer from the Queen's Theatre in Dublin.

There was a reason for this unexpected opening, but it was mercifully hidden from him as he crossed the Irish

Sea. The manager at the Queen's had just dismissed George Vincent, his juvenile lead, who was particularly popular with the regular patrons of the theatre. Vincent's wife had money. Thus, the displaced idol had no need either to crawl to his late employer or to leave Dublin in search of other work. He could afford to stay and see what his successor was like. What was more, he could afford to hire hooligans to interrupt the performance.

For three weeks Irving was received with hoots and hisses every time he appeared in a part formerly played by Vincent. Sometimes the uproar stopped the play. Once he had to advance to the footlights and appeal direct to the audience.

'I should be glad,' he said, 'if you would tell me the reason for this disapprobation. I have frequently appeared in England and Scotland, in London and Edinburgh, with applause, but among a certain few of the audience here I have been denied it. I came among you an entire stranger, I have endeavoured to please you, and really I have been treated by some with anything but courtesy.'

His words drew applause from all parts of the house and for that evening at least the interrupters were silenced. But they renewed their activities on subsequent evenings and were overcome only after a free fight with the police.

Fortunately this Dublin engagement was only a stop-gap. Irving had another already booked in Glasgow. For the next six years he acted there and in other leading cities, Manchester and Liverpool, Oxford and Birmingham. It was in Manchester that he first fell in love.

Nellie Moore was a member of the company there, and

one whom he could admire both as a girl and as an actress. She was beautiful, with a wonderful head of golden hair, intelligent, charming and sympathetic. What was more, she was respectable, a church-goer, and a supporter of good causes. In short, she demonstrated what Irving had so often tried to prove to his mother – that a girl could be on the stage and even (like Nellie) born of stage folk, yet be an admirable member of society. Mrs Brodribb was only one of millions in mid-Victorian England who found this hard to believe.

Nellie lived with her mother. Irving used to walk her home. Sometimes he stayed for one of those late-night suppers at which the professional actor loves to relax after the tensions of the day. He and Nellie grew fond of each other, but there was no talk of marriage. A man could not propose until he had prospects. Irving had none. Nellie's career was more firmly established than his own. Pride and prudence delayed any further development of their friendship, but it continued even when their work took them in different directions.

Irving's arduous ten-year apprenticeship in the provinces ended at last in October, 1866, when he joined a first-class London company at the St James's Theatre, with the additional duties of stage manager. Discerning critics and theatre-goers began to notice him. The novelist George Eliot was among the first to appreciate his special, quite individual talent. Irving had not arrived yet, but success was in view, and Nellie, now playing at the Haymarket a few minutes' walk away, was as delighted as he was. The Moores had a house off Soho

Square, and, as his own parents had gone back to Bristol, Irving had taken bachelor lodgings in Old Quebec Street, near by. With the two homes and the two theatres in the same square mile of the West End, conditions seemed ideal for the old romance to put forth fresh shoots.

Now came one of those real-life coincidences which a good writer scarcely dares to use in fiction.

Clement Scott, the *Sunday Times* dramatic critic, invited Irving to a party. He went to the wrong house. As he stood in the hall, apologizing to the maid for his mistake and listening to her directions for finding Scott's home close by, a tall and striking girl in evening dress came downstairs and gave him a swift glance of recognition. 'Are you not Mr Henry Irving, the actor?' she inquired. Irving bowed and smiled. She introduced herself as Florence O'Callaghan, a keen theatre-goer and a friend of Mr Scott's, to whose party she too was going. As neither her mother nor her sister was accompanying her, and her father, Surgeon General O'Callaghan, was in India, it was the most natural thing in the world that Irving should escort her.

It was perhaps not Miss O'Callaghan but Irving who most needed protection. She was a young woman of relentless determination and she decided almost at once to marry him. She had been flirting mildly with Clement Scott. She used that friendship as a bridge to reach Irving until she knew him well enough for a direct approach. She invited him to dine at her home one Sunday evening with Scott as fellow-guest. Irving could not accept, because of a previous engagement, but she did not relax her efforts. She was infatuated. Her father's disapproval, as she developed her acquaintance with the young actor, only strengthened her resolve. The General, being at the other side of the world, was at a disadvantage. Mrs O'Callaghan, though full of misgivings, could not control her daughter unaided.

Irving too began to imagine himself in love. Inevitably his relationship with Nellie was overshadowed and Nellie seems to have turned her eyes, however regretfully, in another direction. How it would have ended we cannot be sure. In January, 1869, Nellie was taken ill with scarlet fever. Her mother was away in America and Irving was anxious about her. One morning he went round to the house to leave her a bunch of violets, only to see with horror that the blinds were drawn and to be told that she was dead. Thirty-six years later, after his own death, her photograph was found in his pocket book, pasted together back to back with one of himself taken at the same period.

Florence was now pressing for a definite engagement. Her parents yielded reluctantly. Irving's own father was no more enthusiastic – his mother was no longer living. The engagement was announced in April. Florence wanted the wedding as soon as possible, but Irving's London season had ended and, as he explained to her, his summer touring of the provinces would have made a most uncomfortable start for their married life. It was not as though he would be spending a week in each town. It was largely an affair of 'one-night stands'. A typical week's schedule ran: Monday, Gloucester; Tuesday,

Worcester; Wednesday and Thursday, Leicester; Friday, Gloucester; Saturday, Birmingham. Florence agreed to wait until July.

The wedding took place on the 15th, at St Marylebone parish church. None of Irving's family attended and the reception was held, not at the bride's home in Linden Gardens, but at the house of some of Irving's theatrical friends. It was an ill-omened beginning, especially since Florence, much as she enjoyed the theatre, did not in general like theatrical people off the stage. Their late hours and unconventional liveliness offended her.

It is noteworthy that Irving described himself in the marriage register as a 'comedian'. This was how the public still regarded him. But the time was drawing near when his genius for strong drama and tragedy would blaze forth, and when there would be a tendency in some quarters to overlook the great comic gifts which he undoubtedly possessed.

The first year of marriage started auspiciously enough. Florence bore a son, whom they christened Henry Brodribb. Irving, now thirty-two, scored his first real London success in a light comedy, *The Two Roses,* which ran for three hundred nights. This was remarkable at the time, when the modern system of the long run was only beginning to take the place of a frequently changing repertory. It looked as though Irving had achieved financial security at last, just when it was most needed, and that the home he and Florence had set up in Bayswater was safely established.

Worse dangers than money difficulties, however, threatened that home. There was the fundamental clash of temperaments and ways of life. Florence could be cold, biting and disapproving. Irving had the warm, sociable, highly strung nature which so often goes with the actor. He lived at a high pitch of tension before and during his work, and afterwards he must unwind slowly, relaxing over midnight meals, hot punch, and endless gossip. If Florence had hoped to change his habits she was sadly disappointed.

When she and the baby went off to the seaside, Irving rediscovered – and enjoyed – his bachelor liberty. When they came back, the home atmosphere seemed oppressive. He had made allowances for Florence's bad temper before, but the hoped-for improvement had not arrived with the baby. Life became impossible. Irving went off to stay with an actor friend, Montague, who had been his best man at the ill-fated ceremony only fifteen months before. Then, seeing no likelihood of resuming a happy home life, he found himself rooms off Grosvenor Square. There, after Christmas, Florence went to see him and make promises of improvement if only he would return, and with some forebodings he agreed.

The long run of *The Two Roses* came to an end. The summer saw him on tour, as far afield as Ireland, and Florence busy preparing their move to another house in West Brompton. Back in London, Irving signed up with a new management, a remarkable American couple, Mr and Mrs Bateman, who had taken the Lyceum Theatre, off the Strand. The name was, by coincidence, the same as that of the Sunderland theatre in which he had so humbly started his career. The London Lyceum was now to be coupled with the name of Irving as a chapter-heading in the history of the English stage.

When he joined the Batemans they were not doing very well, and business continued to be poor during the first autumn months. Mr Bateman was depressed. Nor did he brighten when Irving suggested that he should put on a melodrama called *The Bells,* about the remorse of a murderer who, haunted by the memory of his undiscovered crime fifteen years before, dreams himself put on trial for it and convicted. The climax comes when he wakes up, imagining the noose about his neck, and dies of heart failure, surrounded by his horrified family.

Bateman did not believe in the play. Irving did. It appealed to him, just as, long ago in his schooldays, the monologue of the murderer's confession had appealed to him as a Speech Day recitation. He could see that, for all the shoddier elements in the plot and language of *The Bells,* there was material from which he could create a powerful theatrical experience. Having won over the dubious manager, he worked on the piece with a thoroughness and thoughtfulness less often given to a production in those days, when the very conception of a 'producer' scarcely existed. *The Bells* was already an adaptation from the French and he felt justified in rewriting much of the English dialogue to heighten the effect he was seeking. When the curtain went up, one Saturday night at the end of November, he had gone far to creating not only the leading character of Mathias, the guilty burgomaster, but the whole production and in a sense the play.

It was a poor house, unprepared for anything unusual, the hardest to grip and stir. But as the play advanced, Irving cast a deepening mesmeric spell over the audience. He turned a sensational melodrama into a psychological study of what was then a novel kind. For the action was on two levels simultaneously – there was the burgomaster's family, cheerfully busy with the practical preparations for his daughter's wedding in the morning, and there was the burgomaster, behaving with outward normality at first but inwardly reliving the crime he had committed long ago. Apart from a spectacular trial scene, in which the lights slowly went up again upon the burgomaster's bedroom to reveal it transformed, in his dream, into a crowded law court, all this had to be conveyed by Irving's speech, look and gesture, without any of the flash-backs and other technical aids with which television has familiarized us today.

He achieved a complete triumph. Not only the ordinary theatre-goers but the most blasé critics were bowled over. *'The play was listened to,'* wrote one, *'with the most breathless attention, and extraordinary applause followed the fall of the curtain. Acting at once so intelligent and so intense has not been seen on the London stage for many years.'* While he and the other journalists were rushing off to write unanimously favourable notices – and in those days the London newspapers were numbered by the dozen – an exhausted but exalted Irving was having to display his versatility by playing Mr Jingle in *Pickwick*, the after-piece.

When at last he could escape from all the congratulations in dressing room and green room and at the stage door, he took Florence on to the customary champagne supper which his friends were giving in their honour. It was like all such parties – excited, exclamatory, exultant. Irving sat at one end of the table, enjoying the sweetness of his first great success. Florence sat at the far end, the skeleton at the feast. Not just the length of the table divided them, but the whole world. She said nothing, beyond suggesting that Irving was talking too much and boring his friends. He was too happy to notice her coldness.

At long last the party ended. The Irvings were put into their hired brougham and sped on their way home. As they approached Hyde Park Corner he put his hand on her arm affectionately and said:

'Well, my dear, we too shall soon have our own carriage and pair!'

'Are you going on,' she answered, 'making a fool of yourself like this all your life?'

For a moment there was silence in the darkness of the brougham. Then Irving's voice rang out so that the driver could hear him above the jingle of harness and the clopping of the hoofs.

'Stop here, please.'

The carriage drew up. Irving stepped out. Without another word he strode away into the darkness, knowing that the Batemans in Kensington would put him up for the rest of the night. He never spoke to Florence again as long as he lived.

.   .   .   .   .

Divorce was rare in those days. Few people even considered it – and the Irvings were not among the few. They remained married in name, but completely separated. When their second son, Laurence, was born shortly afterwards, Irving was not present at the christening. He knew that, with Florence despising the work which was his life, there could be no happiness together. He would support her financially – he was then earning fifteen pounds a week and sent her eight – but he could not share a home with her. He was deeply distressed at the separation from the two little boys, whom Florence taught to despise him as the years went by. His hope was that, when they grew older, they would see his side of the question and that he would have more chance to show himself a good father to them. This hope was fulfilled: long afterwards both sons went on the stage and were proud to act under his management.

Thus ended Irving's one brief attempt to create a home and family life. Thereafter he gave himself up more completely than ever to his work in the theatre. Though he had his hours of relaxation and his many friendships, his story becomes mainly a chronicle of stage appearances.

He turned now to Shakespeare. In 1874 his *Hamlet* ran for two hundred nights, disproving the current theory that 'Shakespeare spells ruin'. Year after year he appeared in a succession of the great roles – Macbeth, Othello, Richard the Third, Shylock. His approach to Shakespeare was novel, and there were still more innovations when, in 1878, he became his own manager at the Lyceum. Now at last he had a free hand in every department. He could enlist painters, composers and historians in mounting those spectacular productions which set the fashion for a generation.

It was not all plain sailing. He met with coldness and criticism in many quarters. His eccentric mannerisms, his dragging walk and strange pronunciations, were easy targets. For all his mastery of characterization he remained always Irving. The general public wished it so. Probably, in the case of the greatest theatrical personalities, they have always wished it so.

He did not confine himself to Shakespeare. He appeared as Cardinal Richelieu, as Charles the First (his costume copied with scholarly accuracy from a Vandyke portrait), as Becket in Tennyson's play of that name. The exhausting role of Mathias was seldom long out of his repertory: the public, especially in the provinces and in America, never ceased to demand *The Bells*. The most noticeable gap in his work was his reluctance to try plays by the new dramatists beginning to batter at the doors of the theatre. During these years the Dickensian London of his youth had been changing into a new city – the London of the eighteen-nineties, with horse buses and the Metropolitan Railway, Gilbert and Sullivan and Oscar Wilde, the Boer War and Bernard Shaw. Shaw, still unrecognized as a playwright, kept up a lively vendetta with Irving. Not even Ellen Terry, Irving's leading lady and a close friend of both men, could bring the two incompatibles together.

Irving stood for a theatre in which the actor, not the author, was supreme. If he did nothing for the struggling dramatists, he did much for his fellow-players. He may not have been the greatest English actor who ever lived, but no other great actor did as much to improve the status of the profession. From boyhood he had challenged the prejudices of people like his mother, opposing them with his own somewhat idealized picture of actors as 'most intellectual', 'gentlemen and scholars', 'companions of the master spirits of the ages'. By the splendour of his example he succeeded to a remarkable extent. Universities gave him honorary degrees for his contribution to the appreciation of Shakespeare. Exclusive clubs elected him to special membership. Religious bodies invited him to speak on the theatre as the ally, not the enemy, of true morality. Finally, in 1895, he was knighted by the Queen, accepting the honour – never conferred on an actor before – as a symbolic recognition of the entire profession. Today we take it as a matter of course that our top cluster of actors and actresses should be knights and dames, but when Irving drove out of the gates of Windsor Castle as Sir Henry it was a milestone in the player's long weary journey from 'rogue and vagabond' to an accepted place in the most respectable society.

Even now, there was no question of resting on his laurels. His work was truly his life. For another ten years he played on, meeting the onset of age, ill health, and managerial difficulties. He finished with the Lyceum in 1902 and his farewell season in London was given at Drury Lane in the early summer of 1905. A farewell tour of the provinces had been abandoned through illness the previous February, just after his sixty-seventh birthday, but on 2 October it was resumed at Sheffield. He was determined not to disappoint the public he had served for almost half a century.

For the second week of the tour he was at Bradford. Shylock on Monday, Becket on Tuesday, Louis the Eleventh on Wednesday, Mathias on Thursday . . . After that performance he collapsed and, when he recovered, he ordered that the scenery and costumes for *The Bells* should be sent back to London. He knew that he would never possess the demonic strength to play that terrifying role again.

Becket was billed for Friday. He seemed better, but he acted with a kind of remote serenity and members of the cast noticed inexplicable little variations in line and business, unknown to the audience but surprising to fellow-actors who knew his normal consistency. His farewell to Rosamund was spoken with unusual emphasis, and when he took leave of Henry the Second he touched the King's hand with his lips, which he had never done before. Later, instead of saying, 'God's will be done', as Tennyson had written, he said, 'God is my judge'. There was a prophetic appropriateness in that the very last words he delivered as an actor were those of the dying Archbishop: 'Into Thy hands, O Lord, into Thy hands'.

An hour later it was all over. A cab had taken him to his hotel. As he entered the hall, he staggered. 'That chair—' he gasped, but he had barely reached it when he slid to the floor. A local doctor came hurrying out of the manager's private room, but was too late to do more than confirm that he was dead.

7. Anna Pavlova, the Solitary Star

'And when I grow up, Mamma, *I* want to be a ballerina too! I want to dance this same role in this very theatre!'

'We shall have to see, Nura, we shall have to see.'

Madame Pavlova had not the heart to dampen the enthusiasm of her eight-year-old daughter as they pushed their way out through the crowded foyer of the Maryinsky Theatre.

It was natural that Nura's great brown eyes should be shining with excitement in her pale oval face – looking more than ever like the dark ripe cherries with which they were sometimes compared – and that her features, always so expressive, should still reflect the emotions of the last few hours.

This visit to the imperial theatre had been planned as a special treat. Poor widow she might be, but Madame Pavlova had always tried to see that her daughter did not miss all the things that belong to childhood – a Christmas tree, an Easter egg, a present or an outing, however inexpensive, at the proper time. Such an outing was this performance of *The Sleeping Beauty*. She had felt sure that the child would respond to the old fairy tale re-enacted by feather-light dancers to Tchaikovsky's music, and she was delighted now with the success of the visit. She had not bargained for Nura's sudden demand to become a ballerina herself; but no doubt it was only what most little girls said after their first visit to the theatre, and in a week or two Nura would have forgotten all about it.

Nura was a pet name. She was really Anna Pavlovna Pavlova, the surname being accented on the first syllable. The middle name was her 'patronymic' or father's name, very important to remember, for it was polite to call friends by their Christian name and patronymic together. Pavlovna meant 'daughter of Pavel' (or Paul) and if Anna had had a brother, instead of being an only child, his middle name would have been Pavlovitch (son of Paul).

Anna was born into the old Russia of the Tsar or Czar, as the Emperor was called by a corruption of the ancient Roman title 'Caesar'. Her birthplace was St Petersburg (now Leningrad) which was then the capital of the immense Russian Empire, larger even than the Soviet Union today, since it included Finland and part of Poland.

St Petersburg was a city of cold classical beauty. Peter the Great had founded it in 1703, building it on piles in the desolate unhealthy marshes where the River Neva split into separate channels to enter the Baltic. He had transferred his court here from Moscow. St Petersburg was to be Russia's 'window on Europe', even though, as a seaport, that window was iced up from Christmas till

April. Peter and his successors had turned a wilderness
of swamps and islets into a superbly laid-out capital with
graceful bridges and embankments and spacious boule-
vards tapering away into the hazy distance, like the
famous Nevsky Prospekt, forty yards wide and running
straight across the centre for two and a half miles. The
skyline of St Petersburg, with its domes and spires and
cupolas gleaming coppery in the sun, was a vision of
incomparable beauty, especially when seen across an
expanse of blue water or snow-covered ice.

Anna was born in this city of splendour on (probably)
January 31, 1882, though the biographies and reference
books disagree confusingly on the day and year. We can
hardly say she 'first saw the light of day', for there would
have been precious little of it at that season. Petersburg
was a foggy place. Ice locked the waterways – each winter
the tram lines were laid across it to the islands. Snow
furred the housetops, jingling sleighs replaced the carriages in the streets, and the sun did little more than peep
briefly above the flat horizon.

St Petersburg was a good place to be rich in – few
better. The Grand Dukes and the rest of high society
lived in luxury. For all the telegraph wires and broad-
gauged railway track leading out of the city into the white
wastes of the Continent, Russia had still barely come out
of the Middle Ages. It was just over twenty years since
the serfs had been set free on the vast estates from which
these aristocrats drew their wealth – serfs like those who
had gained their freedom in England in the days of Robin
Hood. If Russia as a whole was still struggling out of the

Middle Ages, St Petersburg, with its glittering court and military pageantry, had just about attained the stage of Versailles before the French Revolution. But it was 1882 . . .

The Pavlovs were poor, and St Petersburg was not such a good place to be poor in. Behind the façade of palaces and mansions lay crowded tenements, workshops and mills, in which people toiled for long hours and lived in pigsty conditions. The Pavlovs were not as poor as this, but there was no money to spare, especially after Anna's father died when she was only two.

She had been a weakly baby, arriving two months early and needing the utmost care to keep her alive. As she grew up, she had more of the childish ailments than usual – not only measles but diphtheria and scarlatina. When she was four she pulled a table cloth, upsetting the samovar, the copper tea urn in which burning charcoal kept water continually on the boil. The scald marked her left hand for life, but fortunately her face and neck escaped untouched.

It was for the sake of her health that Anna was sent out of the dank city to spend much of her childhood with her beloved grandmother at Ligovo, a summer resort which was then a mere village, seventeen miles from St Petersburg. There, in a typical Russian house of wood, with an upstairs balcony, a neat front fence of palings, and a line of those silver birches which were always to remain her favourite trees, Anna spent her early years rather as Jenny Lind had done, more than half a century before, in another village almost due west across the

Baltic Sea. Anna too loved to explore the countryside, to look for the first snowdrops when the northern winter cracked suddenly into spring, and to go gathering berries, mushrooms, and wild flowers. Here too she acquired her lifelong love of birds and animals. And because she was a Russian child, it was the Russian fairy tales and legends she heard, and the strumming of balalaikas on warm summer evenings, and the deep bass chanting of the Orthodox Church when the bearded priest, or 'pope', led the services on Sundays and festivals.

After those festivals, after a village wedding or any other event which inspired celebration, it was Russian dancing she saw in Ligovo. Dancing was the natural way in which the common people expressed their love of life and their other emotions – it was, for them, like singing for the Welsh. But it was not until the day she went to that performance of *The Sleeping Beauty* at the Maryinsky and saw dancing exalted into the supreme artistry of the ballet that Anna realized what she must do with her life.

Ballet, at this date, was more highly organized in St Petersburg and Moscow than anywhere else in the world. Indeed, by comparison, it scarcely *was* organized elsewhere. In Italy and France, the countries where it had evolved in the seventeenth and eighteenth centuries, it was at a low ebb. England had no ballet of her own, though she occasionally welcomed foreign performers. In most other countries ballet was never seen.

Peter the Great, determined that St Petersburg should

have all the elegances of Western civilization, had been first to introduce the ballet to Russia, and successive tsars had attracted the best foreign teachers. In Anna's childhood these included men like Johanssen, Petipa and Cecchetti.

Christian Johanssen, born in Stockholm in 1817, had been in Petersburg since 1841 – and the incredible old man was still teaching there in 1906. He represented the pure French tradition of the ballet.

Marius Petipa, two years younger and a native of Marseilles, had worked in Russia since 1847 – and *he* went on till his death in 1910. He was responsible for all productions at the Maryinsky Theatre.

Enrico Cecchetti, born in Rome in 1850, belonged to a younger generation, but as the child of ballet dancers he was steeped in the old traditions – in his case the Italian, as distinct from the French. A great dancer (the London *Times* had long ago compared him, in a rather clumsy compliment, with 'a little rubber bouncing ball'), he was equally great as a teacher. Years later he was to teach dancers like Marie Rambert and Ninette de Valois.

Between them, these and other foreigners had transmitted to the Russian ballet everything that was worth learning from the theatres of France and Italy. To these two valuable ingredients was added a third: the natural Russian aptitude, stemming from vigorous folk dances developed down the centuries. 'Vigour' is a word to note. The Russians came of tough peasant stock, used to hard work and a hard climate. The male dancers were athletic.

Men were not eyed askance, as they sometimes used to be in the West, for taking up what was mistakenly imagined to be an unmanly art. With such human material the foreign teachers could achieve results impossible in their own lands.

The Russian ballet had other special advantages in those days. It was able to enlist first-rate composers – Petipa had interested Tchaikovsky in writing music for the ballet. It had an assured public of season ticket holders, who not only made it fashionable and financially sound but (because they really knew about the ballet) provided that stimulating, informed criticism which alone is useful to the artist. Anna herself, many years later, used to sigh for the knowledgeable audiences of Petersburg. The generous applause of Londoners and New Yorkers would have been sweeter if she could have relied upon them to notice faults. Acutely self-critical, she got no pleasure from being praised when she knew that she had fallen short of her best.

Finally, the Russian ballet had the initial asset of its own school, under the Tsar's protection and patronage. This was the school which, from the first day when she was entranced by *The Sleeping Beauty*, Anna Pavlova was determined to enter.

She had to be patient for two years. Ten was the age for admission. Her mother dreaded lest disappointment should wait at the end of it all. Money was not the problem: if accepted, a child was maintained by the school. But there was keen competition and the chances were ten

to one against acceptance. For Anna they were probably
worse, for there was a strict medical examination and she
was still a fragile-looking child.

The day came. They reported to the school, which was
housed in the palatial building containing also the central
offices of the five imperial theatres and the residence of
the princely director. There seemed to be hundreds of
other girls – there were in fact about one hundred for the
eight places available – and Anna's dark eyes rounded
with apprehension as she surveyed all the expensive
dresses of her rivals. Mamma had done her best. The
child knew she looked neat and clean, that her long hair
was well brushed and tidily plaited, but she must appear
insignificant against these exquisitely turned out young
ladies.

The examiners, however, a jury of the directorate,
teaching staff and eminent dancers, were far too experienced to be influenced by any party frock, however
elegant. They looked for the basic physical attributes
which were the necessary foundation for a dancer. Before
them, for a few brief moments, was just another ten-year-
old, with a pale, serious oval face, aquiline nose, and the
high cheekbones of the Slav. How much more could they
see – then? Later, the critics were to wax lyrical over
the slender torso, the lovely arms, the well-modelled legs,
the slim but strong ankles, the superb and unique
development of the instep, and all the other components
of a 'body ideally formed for dancing'. How many of
these could the examiners detect in 1892? Could they see
the promise in the poise of that neat dark head on a neck

so truly swanlike that it is for ever associated with the swan?

All we know is that the examiners saw enough to convince them that one of the coveted places should be awarded to Anna Pavlova. The doctors confirmed that the child, though thin by the substantial standards of Russian girlhood, was healthy enough to take the course. Anna hugged her mother. She was 'in'.

The school day began at eight o'clock in the morning when a bell roused the girls in their dormitory. They had to wash, dress in their blue uniforms with white aprons, plait their hair, and hurry into the chapel, where a tiny red light shone like a ruby in front of the icon, a sacred painting with embellishments of precious metal which served as a focus for their prayers. Religious feeling was deeply seated in the Russian character – though critics might often complain that it was mere superstition. Few of the young dancers in those days would have made a first entrance on the stage without piously crossing themselves as they waited in the wings.

Breakfast was at nine, a simple affair of bread, butter and tea. Then it was time for dancing lessons in the lofty room which looked bigger because of the huge mirrors. Anna and the other new girls practised first, then their seniors, group by group. And from the walls the portraits of bygone Tsars and Tsarinas looked down, one hoped approvingly.

Midday brought lunch, literally 'the second breakfast'. A short walk followed, then more lessons till four, then a good dinner, starting with the great plate of soup without which no dinner would be dinner to a Russian. Now at last the girls had a little time to themselves, but very soon they were called to fencing classes, music lessons, and perhaps rehearsals of some performance that was being planned. Supper was at eight, bed at nine.

It was a full day, but not a hard one, for discipline was reasonable and the pupils were enthusiastic. They had to master all the steps of the classical ballet and to learn not only the minuet and the mazurka but various historical dances and the national ones of Hungary, Spain and other countries. As Anna worked her way up through the school she found that the seniors had to fit in many hours of private practice as well. Even so, she was sometimes impatient with the leisurely tempo of the seven-year course. She felt that she could have covered it in five years. Some schools did.

There were occasional high-lights. When she was fourteen there was a state visit from the German Emperor, or 'Kaiser' (another variant of 'Tsar' and 'Caesar'), and there was great excitement in the school when it was known that they were to take part in a gala performance in his honour. To make matters even better, this was to be at Peterhof, the imperial summer residence, a kind of seaside Versailles on the southern shore of the Gulf of Finland, eighteen miles from the capital. Peterhof had fountains and statues and lakes with islands. One of these islands served as stage for the dancers and they were watched by the two emperors and an audience glittering and rippling with jewels and medals like the waters of the lake which twinkled between. This was in the summer, when even North Russia is hot and the sun sinks so briefly beneath the horizon that there is hardly any darkness, only a magical silvery dimness known as 'the white nights'.

Anna had a modest role as a water lily, but she never forgot that evening. Nor did the Kaiser. He mentioned it to her eighteen years afterwards.

As time went by, Anna's talent was remarkable enough to attract the special attention of her principal teacher, Pavel Gerdt, himself a fine dancer and a pupil of the veteran Johanssen. He saw that, though she had the ideal physical equipment, her frailty must still be reckoned with. It was most important that her training should be developed along the right lines. But she was much more than a fortunate assemblage of perfect physical features and proportions, added to technique. She had a soul, a spiritual quality, which showed in her changing expressions, in the faintest quiver of her fingertips. She had the magnetism which marked the true star in the theatre and enabled her to hold the stage alone.

For that reason Anna soon achieved an unusual privilege: from her first professional appearance at the Maryinsky Theatre in the summer of 1899 she was assigned small parts and never had to serve an apprenticeship in the *corps de ballet*. If she had done so, it is possible that she would have developed a different conception of ballet as a collective effort, in which solo dancers and chorus combined with choreographer and composer,

producer and designer, conductor and orchestra, to create
an artistic whole greater than the sum of all its separate
parts. Perhaps nothing could have changed her nature.
She was an individualist. Now, at seventeen, she could
no longer merge herself into a chorus of water lilies or
dryads. She must be Sister Anne in *Blue Beard*, Juanita in
Don Quixote, the Lilac Fairy in *The Sleeping Beauty*.

On one unforgettable evening she had to dance before
the Tsar in his private theatre. This formed part of the
Hermitage Palace, the vast imperial museum and art
gallery, connected by a passageway with the Winter
Palace and overlooking the Neva very much as the
Louvre runs along the Seine embankment in Paris. The
Tsar of all the Russias, as he was grandly known when
he was not spoken of with simple affection as 'the Little
Father', was a kindly, bearded man in his thirties, closely
resembling a first cousin who in a few more years would
be crowned King George the Fifth of England. He sat
there that night, surrounded by the splendours of an
empire which was soon to pass away, and mercifully unaware of the fate in store for himself, his wife, and the
children to whom he was so devoted.

Meanwhile, if the rulers of Russia could not see where
the country was going, a single-minded hard-working
ballet dancer could hardly be blamed for noticing little
outside the theatre. Poverty and misery were part of
Russian life: one was sorry, naturally, and gave a small
coin to a beggar, if one could spare it, just as one did not
pass a church without making the sign of the cross. It was
terrible, of course, to hear of strikes and hunger riots, and

the soldiers shooting people down or the fierce Cossacks riding their horses on to the pavement and lashing right and left with their *knouts*. But order must be preserved or decent folk would not sleep safe in their beds. Certainly, when Anna and the other girls chattered in the dressing rooms of the Maryinsky, it is unlikely that they were often complaining about the censorship of books and newspapers, the secret police, or the lack of democracy as it existed in Western countries. And we may be quite sure that none of them had ever heard of a man named Ulyanov, just released from exile in Siberia, now plotting abroad and soon to be known as Lenin; or of a Georgian named Dzhugashvili (later Stalin), recently expelled from theological college and now working underground in the Socialist movement; or of a little peasant boy named Nikita Khrushchev, who would follow them in turn, just as they would follow Nicholas the Second, as the foremost man in Russia.

Anna had no thought for anything but the ballet. Her early success did not turn her head. 'Success?' she once said in the years afterwards. 'What is it? I do not find it in the applause of the theatre. It lies rather in the satisfaction of accomplishment.'

She was a perfectionist. She must leave nothing unlearnt. One summer she used her vacation to make the long journey to Milan and see if there was anything fresh to learn from the land in which ballet had originated. For two years she took special lessons from Eugenia Sokolova, the former prima ballerina at the Maryinsky. In 1905 – twenty-three now, and a *première danseuse* – she met

Cecchetti in Moscow and persuaded the Italian *maestro,* the 'little rubber bouncing ball' who was still so full of life, to come to Petersburg and coach her.

That year even ballet dancers could not be unaware of politics. It began with a Sunday afternoon in January, when nearly a quarter of a million people marched through the streets of the capital, converging from all directions on the vast snow-covered square in front of the Winter Palace. It was a peaceful, respectful multitude, led by a much-loved priest and including thousands of women and children. They carried sacred icons and portraits of the Emperor, they sang *God Save the Tsar.* The petition they brought asked for an eight-hour day, a minimum wage of a rouble (or about fifty cents) a day, a ban on overtime, and some form of Parliament to give the people a little share in the government. The Tsar was not there to receive the petition. He had moved out to one of his country houses and in fact, for the rest of his reign, he never came back to live in the Winter Palace. Perhaps the place was too haunted. For in his absence, that Sunday afternoon, the guards opened fire on the crowd at point-blank range. Over five hundred people were killed and thousands wounded. This terrible beginning to 1905 was continued with the assassination of the Governor of Moscow in front of the Kremlin, strikes, arrests, naval mutinies, and the murder of about fifteen hundred government officials in different parts of the country. Petersburg had a general strike, a complete stoppage of all normal life. Even the *corps de ballet* went on strike. Red flags waved in the streets. The workmen in the different trades sent delegates to a central committee called a *soviet*. The 1905 Revolution petered out, but it had served as a dress rehearsal for 1917.

For Anna 1905 was the year in which Michael Fokine, a brilliant dancer and choreographer who had been two years her senior at the ballet school, created a new dance for her to perform at a charity show. It was conceived hurriedly but not carelessly. At twenty-five a young artist's imagination gushes with the force and splendour of a fountain – and this Fokine was the choreographer of *Les Sylphides*, *Petrouchka*, and the *Prince Igor* dances. Like most brilliant young men, he was afire to do something different, and this not very important assignment for an old fellow-student gave him an opportunity. He created *The Dying Swan*, using the music of Saint-Saëns. It was revolutionary in its conception, for, as he said, it was 'a dance of the whole body and not of the limbs only, appealing not merely to the eye but to the emotions and the imagination'. It was the right dance for Pavlova – a supreme solo effort, making the most of her physical appearance and giving full scope for her uncanny gift of identification, of becoming, for a few transfigured minutes, the character she portrayed. As Arnold Haskell was to write later, in *Balletomania*: 'Her face . . . could assume beauty at will; so that there was not one Pavlova but many; a gypsy, a dying delirious woman, a coquette.' He might have added 'a flower, a dragonfly, a swan'. It was the role of the swan that was to be specially associated with Anna for the rest of her life. It was

Fokine's creation that her public demanded everywhere.

The next year, 1906, saw her promoted to prima ballerina. In 1907 she made her first foreign tour – to Stockholm, where the delighted King Oscar gave her the Swedish Order of Artistic Merit, then to Copenhagen, Berlin and Prague. The following year saw her back in Prague and conquering new audiences in Leipzig and Vienna. In 1909 it was the turn of Paris.

Here she appeared twice with the newly formed Diaghilev Company. They were presenting a mixed season of ballet and opera. To the sophisticated Parisian audiences who had never seen a performance in Moscow or St Petersburg, the vitality and colour of the Diaghilev productions came as a sensational experience.

Sergei Diaghilev was a strange, fanatical character whom Anna had known in Petersburg. Ten years older than she, he was a country nobleman's son who had come to the university to study law but with a private ambition to become a composer. He had haunted the theatres and the concert halls, he had made friends with artists and writers, but for a long time he had shown little interest in the ballet, being occupied in running exhibitions and founding a journal called *The World of Art*. It was his co-editor, Benois, a ballet enthusiast, who aroused him to the possibilities of that medium, and it soon became the dominant passion of his life. He secured a post at the Maryinsky and was entrusted with a production of Delibes's *Sylvia,* but his unusual ideas and dictatorial manner brought the indignant dancers to the verge of a strike, and as Diaghilev would not budge an inch, he was dismissed. After that, he had no hope of realizing his ideas in Russia, and some years later he launched his own company in Paris, where he had already put on Russian art exhibitions, concerts and operas. Now, for the next twenty years, until he died in Venice in 1929, he made the Ballets Russes world famous.

It was a brilliant company he had assembled for that first season. Besides Anna there were Tamara Karsavina, who was later to settle in England and coach Margot Fonteyn, and Nijinsky, greatest of all male dancers. Michael Fokine came as choreographer and Cecchetti as ballet master. The repertory included the newly created *Les Sylphides*.

Anna's connection with the company was short. She and Diaghilev were poles apart. He had no use for the 'star' system. Aloof and arrogant, he expected absolute obedience from his artists: often he got almost worship. His aim was to cater to a cultured public, offering them the finest dancing, music and décor attainable by a fusion of the arts. Anna herself loved to dance for that same public, knowledgeable people who appreciated the finer points of ballet, but she was prepared also to travel to the ends of the earth, introducing the art where it had never been seen before, and dancing wherever the minimum facilities were to be found. To her the dance was everything. The music, the décor, everything else was secondary. And her taste in these matters was more conventional than his – she had no sympathy with much of the new trend in music and painting at the dawn of the twentieth century. Ballet owes an incalculable debt to both Pavlova and Diaghilev, but no one company was big enough to hold them both for long. It is said that he never forgave her for succeeding without him; and she in turn saw the world divided into two camps, hers and Diaghilev's.

It was about now that her life became closely linked with that of her future husband, Victor Dandré, originally a Russian landowner and a fellow law student of Diaghilev's, whom she had first known in Petersburg. Some say that Dandré was her evil genius, tempting her to leave Diaghilev and fritter away her great gifts on second-rate material. Others say that his practical abilities were the ideal counterpart to her talents and made her success possible. Certainly he managed all her business affairs, planned tours, carried on her correspondence, steered her through press conferences, shielded her from tiresome callers, and in every way helped her to save her energies for her real work. As she became more famous, and it was likely that some day a book might be written about her, she said that he ought to be the one to write it, because he knew and understood her best. Soon after her death he did in fact write such a book, *Anna Pavlova in Art and Life*, but it gave away scarcely one detail about himself. Its countless illustrations included only a single glimpse of a big man sitting on a garden seat at their house in Hampstead, with a relaxed Anna leaning back, her head upon his shoulder.

Hampstead, because soon London was to become her home for the rest of her life.

Her first glimpse of London came in 1909, when she crossed from Paris to dance at a private party in honour of King Edward the Seventh and Queen Alexandra. In the following April she appeared in public at the Palace Theatre. She brought a company of twelve, the biggest team of Russian dancers the Londoners had yet seen, though Lydia Kyasht and Tamara Karsavina had both danced in London a year or two earlier. Pavlova and her Greek-god-like partner, Mikhail Mordkin, gave the British a fresh and exciting revelation of what Russian ballet could do. Their stormily passionate *Autumn Bacchanal* and her own haunting and pathetic *Swan* were still the talk of the town when, three weeks later, the King's death closed the theatres and filled the black-edged newspapers with other matters.

Anna now crossed the Atlantic and danced *Coppélia* in New York. April 1911 found her back at the Palace Theatre, almost a year to the day since her début there, in a London excitedly preparing for George the Fifth's coronation in June. Diaghilev brought his company to Covent Garden for that brilliant season, and the rift between him and Anna was not yet so deep as to prevent her joining them. She took the principal roles in *Les Sylphides* and *Giselle*. Many thought *Giselle* was her greatest role and gave the fullest scope to her powers as an actress.

Apart from this season with Diaghilev, Anna's life was beginning to fall into a pattern. She toured, making a short annual appearance in London. Between tours she went back to Petersburg, driven by her quest for perfec-

tion, and took a refresher course with her old teachers at
the Maryinsky.

London, however, was her base and soon she began to
include more and more English girls in her company.
This dated from an unfortunate incident when Mikhail
Mordkin lifted her incorrectly and in a fit of anger she
slapped his face on the stage. Mordkin promptly left the
company. All the Polish girls and some of the Russians
walked out after him. Anna was able to replace her male
partner and for the rest of her career she continued to get
men dancers almost exclusively from Russia, but it was
not so easy to recruit enough girls for what was a mainly
female company. She found English girls unexpectedly
good and developed a preference for them. Their sense of
discipline appealed to her. Only their emotional restraint
was sometimes a handicap. 'Why do you always go about
with your lips tucked in, expressing nothing?' she would
demand. 'Cry, when you want to cry! Laugh, when you
want to laugh!'

In 1912 Anna and her husband bought the house at
Hampstead and sent to Russia for their possessions. Ivy
House had once belonged to the painter, Turner. Standing in two acres of garden in North End Road, in a
Hampstead which was then still something of a hilltop
village overlooking the city, it seemed to the Russian
couple a typical English country house. Anna loved the
flowers and shrubs, the close-mown grass sloping down
to the circular pool, the fountain, the background tapestry
of mighty trees. She liked to recline in a hammock, to
serve tea to her friends in a tent, to sit on the ground with

her mother in the midst of the croquet hoops, feeding the fantail pigeons which came fluttering to her call. Even at one o'clock in the morning, back from the theatre, she liked to wander round the garden before going to bed.

Animals were another delight. She owned a succession of dogs, a Siamese cat, a peacock, parrots and flamingos. The conservatory housed an ever-increasing collection of brightly coloured birds, many acquired after she began to tour in tropical countries. And in time, most appropriate of all, there were swans gliding on the miniature lake, swans with which she developed an uncanny friendship, especially 'Jack', who would sit in her lap and curve his long white neck around her own in gentle affection.

The house itself was spacious – today it forms part of Manor House Hospital. Its fourteen rooms included a lofty galleried hall, which, with its long mirror, practice bar, and grand piano in one corner, served as her studio. There were fine dry cellars under the whole building which provided ideal storage for the costumes, wigs, and music library of her entire company. When Pavlova was at home she liked to get away from the 'international' cooking which was so much the same in all hotels, trains and ships throughout the world, and go back to Russian food – coarse black bread, sturgeon, rissoles in sour cream, and honey or jam not with but *in* her tea. Whether at home or on tour, she always insisted on keeping up the old Russian festivals. At Easter there must be red-painted eggs, sweet buns called *kulichi*, and the cheese cake called *pascha*. Wherever they were at Christmas (and only once were they in England), Victor must somehow discover a Christmas tree. It was particularly difficult once in Burma, but in the end he managed to obtain a diminutive fir tree. Never, though, did they have children of their own to deepen the happiness of the Christmas season.

July, 1914, found the company in Berlin. The Kaiser received Anna most amiably, told her how he remembered the ballet on the lake at Peterhof eighteen years before, and was incredulous when she replied that she had taken part in it as a water lily. This must have been one of the last evenings of the glittering old world into which she had grown up – the world of empires and plumes and prancing horses and fantastic uniforms. By the end of that month the guns had opened and an ugly new age of field-grey and khaki had begun. The Kaiser was at war with the Tsar. Anna and her company packed hurriedly and caught one of the last trains through Belgium. They were just in time. The German armies were close behind them, sweeping into Belgium, and the dancers were scarcely over the sea before Britain was countering with a declaration of war on Germany.

Throughout the four and a half years of that first World War Anna and Victor toured North and South America. Once on that side of the Atlantic, it was not easy to return. The German submarines were sinking liners – the torpedoed *Lusitania* went down with nearly twelve hundred passengers and crew – and in those more civilized days people were not used to the idea that any-one but soldiers and sailors should perish in a war. Anna felt a great responsibility for the girls in her company. Just as she watched over their welfare in peace time, rather like a strict but benevolent headmistress, now in wartime she was not going to risk their lives on the Atlantic.

In 1917 came news of the Russian Revolution. First the Tsar's absolute power was taken from him by a liberal government, then this government was in turn overthrown by the soviets, led by Lenin and his fellow-Communists, or Bolsheviks. Anna read in the papers of fighting in the streets and squares she had known in her childhood and of a battle for possession of the Winter Palace. Rumours and refugees came pouring out of Russia. Soon the Revolution – which so many Western people had welcomed as good and necessary – began to take on an uglier look. The Tsar and his family were brutally executed, their bodies thrown down a mine shaft. Grand Dukes and generals who led loyal armies against the new Soviet government were defeated one by one, and so were the British and other foreign expeditions sent into Russia to help them.

When people asked Anna where she would finally settle down, she used to smile and answer, 'Oh, somewhere in Russia.' But as the nineteen-twenties went on it became obvious that the Russia she had known was gone, never to return. How would she like the new Russia? Humbly born though she was, she had grown up as a daughter of the Imperial Ballet, under the sheltering wings of the Tsarist eagle, knowing little of the peasants and workers whose desperation had destroyed the old régime.

Meanwhile, she was still a youngish woman. Life stretched before her. Anything might happen in another twenty years. Ivy House, joyfully regained after the end of the war, was all the home she needed at present. In any case she was mostly on tour.

In those years she was a sort of missionary for ballet, carrying it into the farthest corners of the world and creating a public for it which had never existed before. Theodore Stier, her Austrian musical director for sixteen years, reckoned that they travelled 300,000 miles in that period, and that he conducted 3,650 performances as well as 2,000 rehearsals. She was tireless in practice and rehearsal. 'The true artist,' she always said, 'must sacrifice herself to her art.' But she found energy to enjoy the wonders of the world in passing. She would get on a camel to visit the pyramids, scramble up the Sphinx, tramp the art galleries of Florence and Siena, take a boat to view the riverside glory of Benares. Java, the Taj Mahal, Yellowstone Park: she wanted to see everything, from Amalfi to the Andes. It was a high sunny valley in California, carpeted with golden-yellow poppies, which she came upon with delighted surprise after being nearly snowed up in the mountain pass, that gave her the inspiration for her dance, *The California Poppy*.

She made new friends and met old ones on these journeys. There were affectionate reunions with her beloved teacher, Cecchetti, in Milan. In South America she so impressed a bishop that, when she sailed away, he wrote to the ship's captain, commending her and her young ladies to his special protection. In Shanghai, then full of Russian refugees, her dancing inspired a child named Tamara Toumanova, who as a result made her way to Paris and became herself a brilliant ballerina. But nowhere more than in England, her adopted home, did Anna's work bear fruit.

Much progress was made between 1920 and 1930. Marie Rambert, a Polish pupil of Cecchetti's, started her school in London and then her Ballet Club. Great names made their first appearance in the public eye – Frederick Ashton, the Irish Ninette de Valois, Constant Lambert the composer, and others, not forgetting Arnold Haskell, the writer whose chronicles and criticism have done so much to educate the British public in a better understanding of the art. Haskell, later to become director of the Royal Ballet School, was a prime mover in founding the Camargo Society, named after the great French dancer of the eighteenth century, and formed to further the cause of ballet in England.

Anna's pioneer efforts had created the favourable climate in which all this could flourish. Her company and often the material she used might be open to criticism – too much was mediocre by the higher standards which were being set – but her individual artistry remained supreme. She was still under fifty, still dancing with the ethereal grace which had entranced the London audiences twenty years before.

The world was never to see the fading of her star. In January, 1931, on her way from a brief holiday in the south of France before starting a fresh tour in Holland, she caught a chill which developed into pleurisy by the time she reached her hotel at The Hague. Victor had been called back to London on business but luckily he joined her later that same day. It was a brief illness. The inflammation spread to the second lung, the heart showed alarming signs of weakness. On the evening of the sixth day Anna opened her eyes and spoke faintly to her maid, Marguerite, who had scarcely left her side.

'Get out my swan costume . . .'

She said nothing after that. Midnight struck. Half an hour later she died.

She was mourned in every country in which she had ever danced. There was a moving funeral service in London. A choir of Russian exiles sang the chants of the Orthodox Church in which she had been brought up, and the coffin was draped with the old imperial Russian flag which was the only one she had ever known. Perhaps the newly formed Camargo Society paid her the most fitting tribute, when, at their Sunday evening recital two days after her death, they played the *Dying Swan* music to an empty stage. They knew (what later ambitious dancers and students would be slow to learn) that Anna Pavlova had *been* the swan, and for those who had seen her dance the role there could never be another. One such admirer, Dermot Spence, summed up in some verses what was in all their minds at that performance:

A moment's pause before the show goes on,
A minute's breath before we turn the page:
The dying flutter of an unseen Swan,
The weeping music and the empty stage.

. . . an empty stage . . . and yet the whole house sees
In the blue limelight more than vacant air:
A whispered hint of shadow draperies—
And surely Pavlova is dancing there.

Suggestions for Further Reading

Readers wishing to read any of these life stories in fuller detail will find that there is a wealth of biographies, memoirs, and more general histories. Of the innumerable volumes consulted in the writing of this little book the following have been particularly helpful: *Marlowe and His Circle* by F. S. Boas, 1929; *The Tragical History of Christopher Marlowe* by J. Bakeless, 1942; *Christopher Marlowe* by P. H. Kocher, 1947; and *The Muses' Darling* by C. Norman, 1948. *Molière, His Life and Works* by J. Palmer, 1930, and *Molière, The Comic Mask* by D. B. Wyndham Lewis, 1959. *Portrait of Mrs Siddons* by Naomi Royde-Smith, 1933; and *Mrs Siddons, Tragic Actress* by Yvonne Ffrench, 1954. *Giuseppe Verdi: Life and Works* by F. Toye, 1931; and *Verdi* by Dyneley Hussey, 1948. *Jenny Lind* by Joan Bulman, 1956; and *Memoir of Madame Jenny Lind–Goldschmidt* by H. Scott-Holland and W. S. Rockstro, 1891. *Henry Irving: The Actor and His World* by Laurence Irving, 1951; and *Henry Irving* by Gordon Craig, 1930. *Anna Pavlova in Art and Life* by V. Dandré, 1932; and *Anna Pavlova* by C. W. Beaumont, 1932.

·   ·   ·   ·

The author is indebted to Mr Dermot Spence for permission to quote from his poem on Pavlova, originally printed in Arnold Haskell's *Balletomania*.